NORMATIVE DECISION MAKING

SHEEN KASSOUF
School of Social Sciences
University of California

PRENTICE-HALL FOUNDATIONS OF ADMINISTRATION SERIES
HERBERT A. SIMON, series editor

PRENTICE-HALL, INC., Englewood Cliffs, New Jersey

PRENTICE-HALL INTERNATIONAL, INC., London
PRENTICE-HALL OF AUSTRALIA, PTY. LTD., Sydney
PRENTICE-HALL OF CANADA, LTD., Toronto
PRENTICE-HALL OF INDIA PRIVATE LTD., New Delhi
PRENTICE-HALL OF JAPAN, INC., Tokyo

© 1970 by Prentice-Hall, Inc., Englewood Cliffs, New Jersey

Printed in the United States of America

P–13–623686–3
C–13–623694–4
Library of Congress Catalog Card No.: 75–115835

Current printing:
10 9 8 7 6 5 4 3 2 1

FOREWORD

This volume is aimed at providing a clear and concise introduction to modern ways of conceptualizing the decision-making process—ways that have provided powerful analytic tools for the complex decision-making tasks of today's managers and organizations. Detailed treatments of the new decision-making techniques are available in several textbooks, but the student who is introduced to these ideas for the first time, and especially the student who does not intend to become a specialist in operations research, wants initially an overview of basic concepts and ideas. It is such an overview that Professor Kassouf provides in this volume.

The volume was designed to be usable as the text in that section of an introductory course on foundations of management or administration devoted to decision making, and it was developed within the limits of size and technical level appropriate to that use. In time, we hope that it will be incorporated in a series treating in a similar manner a whole range of basic management concepts— a series that can serve as the text material for a full semester course on foundations of administration. Since Professor Kassouf's manuscript provides an exceptionally clear and useful introduction to normative theories of decision making, usable as an independent unit in a variety of contexts, we have thought that it should be made available to teachers and students as promptly as possible, and without waiting for other units of the prospective series.

The interest and practical importance of normative decision theory is not limited to management situations where we can actually employ formal techniques like linear programming or Bayesian decision theory. Even in areas where we will continue, for a long time, to make our decisions in less formal and more qualitative fashion, the *ideas* underlying the formal theory—ideas of utility, constraints, probability, and so on—will be of great value in helping us to think clearly about complex problems. Formal decision theory is the logical foundation for a set of powerful mathematical techniques; but it is also a mode of thought —a point of view—that can illuminate many situations where we may not see our way to the literal application of formal techniques.

Decision theory today continues to develop vigorously and rapidly. New approaches—for example, so-called "heuristic" methods—are attracting much attention and study. In this volume, Professor Kassouf has not undertaken to depict this changing scene in detail, but rather to focus on fundamental ideas that will remain central to an understanding of the decision-making process, whatever path new developments may take. The student whose interest in decision making is sparked by studying this introduction will find no dearth of new roads to explore and new worlds to conquer.

HERBERT A. SIMON

Pittsburgh, Pennsylvania

CONTENTS

INTRODUCTION
ONE 1

DECISION MAKING
UNDER
CERTAINTY
TWO 5

strategies, outcomes, and certainty 6
rational decision makers 7

a consumer's decision problem   8
utility functions   13
an example of utility maximization   15
more decision making under certainty   17
summary   21
PROBLEMS   22
REFERENCES   22

DECISION MAKING WITH OBJECTIVE PROBABILITIES

THREE   25

objective probabilities   26
the decision situation   26
expected value of a strategy   28
the petersburg paradox   29
normative decisions with objective probabilities   30
cardinal versus ordinal utility   36
resolving the petersburg paradox   38
PROBLEMS   42
REFERENCES   43

DECISION MAKING WITH SUBJECTIVE PROBABILITIES

FOUR   45

subjective probability   46
the existence of subjective probabilities   47
summary   52
PROBLEM   53
REFERENCES   54

AN APPLICATION
PORTFOLIO
SELECTION
FIVE   55

selecting a portfolio from a universe of two securities   56
efficient portfolios   61
PROBLEMS   64
REFERENCES   64

IN THE ABSENCE
OF PROBABILITIES
SIX   65

the principle of indifference   66
the maxi-min criterion   68
the maxi-max criterion   68
the hurwicz-optimism index   69
the savage regret criterion   70
PROBLEMS   73
REFERENCES   73

FURTHER
GENERALIZATIONS
SEVEN   75

strategy selection under conflict   75
nonzero-sum games   78
collective decision making   81
PROBLEMS   86
REFERENCES   86

INTRODUCTION
CHAPTER ONE

As free men we are forced to link desires with capabilities. We may do this impulsively or unconsciously but, willy-nilly, decisions must be made. How *should* an individual or group decide between alternative courses of action? This question will be explored in this book.

How decisions *should* be made, as opposed to how decisions *are* made, involves *normative* analysis. A few decades ago many social scientists became disenchanted with normative theories because they seemed "unscientific." For example, when an economist ad-

vises that a tariff should be imposed on automobiles, he is expressing a value judgment that discriminates against consumers in favor
of the auto industry. But the economist has no expertise in forming
value judgments—his competence as an *economist* does not make
his preferences superior to a layman's. And so it was said that
normative, or prescriptive theories should be abandoned by social
scientists because values are not subject to scientific analysis.

If a normative theory specifies values or goals, then there may
be no "experts." If, however, goals, values, or desires are *given*,
then decision makers may usefully exploit "experts" who can
instruct them how they *should* behave. This will be our starting
point: we assume that the decision maker starts with explicit
values or goals and that he is to decide how to make the best
choice among available alternatives. This assumption eliminates
much of the vitality of human behavior, because desires are almost
never "given" and are seldom clear. The "value [of intellect] to
any man lies in the speed and strength with which it can help him
to clarify his desire and to act or build according to its dictates." [1]

Some believe that institutional forces twist and distort an individual's preferences so that he no longer knows what is "good."
John Kenneth Galbraith, in *The Affluent Society*, argues that
advertising in our society tends to lead people away from their
self-interest, implying that some of us are better judges than others
concerning goals and desires—a proposition readily acceptable by
most when considering adults versus children or the mentally
incompetent. But this dangerous proposition has too often led to
rule by elites who eventually abused their power. In this book we
sidestep this issue; we pretend that the decision maker knows what
is "best."

Even if we assume that desires are given, we shall have to justify
the statement: You *should* do this to achieve your goal. The
justification sometimes takes the form that a "rational" person
would do this or that. This leads to the question: What do we

[1] Jacques Barzun, *The House of Intellect* (New York: Harper & Row,
    Publishers, 1959), p. 169.

mean by "rational"? We shall show that if preferences are given and if a few assumptions (or axioms) are valid for a decision maker, then logical consequences will dictate his behavior if he does not wish to act illogically. We will call this behavior *rational*.

By a *normative theory* we mean a theory that prescribes how decisions should be made, given goals and values. By *rational behavior* we mean behavior that is logically consistent. Thus, to say that goals cannot be established scientifically, or that the theories are "value free" are not valid objections to the theories we present.

We begin in the simplest of all worlds—the never-never land of complete certainty, where each decision maker knows precisely the consequence attached to every course of action available to him. We then move to situations that are best evident in the casino; each consequence cannot be known in advance, but we can place definite probabilities on the possible consequences. Moving still closer to the real world, we next consider decision situations in which either the probabilities associated with the outcomes are a matter of individual judgment, or no judgment at all can be made about them. Along the way we consider a specific application of decision making to portfolio selection. Further on we examine decision making under conflict, and finally, collective decision making.

The treatment of these topics is neither completely rigorous nor completely intuitive but somewhere between these poles. Rigor was traded for informality to the point where (the author hopes) a beginner's understanding will be optimized. Although much use is made of symbols, the reader only needs knowledge of differential calculus.

Each chapter could easily be expanded into a large volume. The main purpose of this work is not to treat any one topic in detail, but to show the framework connecting a number of areas in modern decision making.

At least one major area of decision theory has been omitted entirely, situations in which the set of alternatives is not clearly defined but must be found or designed. Until recently, this has been a major soft spot in the state of the art. This problem is now under concerted attack (see Ref. 8, Chap. 7).

*   *   *

I am deeply grateful to Professor Herbert A. Simon for his meticulous reading of the entire manuscript and his many useful comments. He is not to be implicated for remaining errors.

DECISION MAKING UNDER CERTAINTY

CHAPTER TWO

A decision situation exists if one must choose among alternative courses of action. For those of us who believe that the future is not completely predetermined, decision situations dominate our lives: of those schools that will accept me, in which shall I enroll; of those girls who will say "yes," which shall I marry; of those jobs offered to me, which shall I take; of all the available houses, which shall I buy; etc. These decisions are often made impulsively, whimsically or, in some cases, after deliberate thought. In this chapter we begin to answer the question, "How *should* decisions be made?" To erase the illusion of omnipotence, we stress at the outset that we will only advise the decision maker if he is rational and if he can reveal to us his values, terms which we now try to define.

strategies, outcomes, and certainty

Let us denote the courses of action, or strategies, in any given situation by $S_1, S_2, \ldots, S_n$ and the possible outcomes by $C_1, C_2, \ldots, C_r$. Note that several strategies may have the same outcome. Strategies are means to ends; they interest us only because they lead to goals that satisfy our desires. (Desires need not be selfish or hedonistic. A parent's desire to send a son to college could involve working long, hard hours.)

We can always define an outcome so that it contains all the aspects that will add or detract from our desires. For instance, a strategy available to me in a given situation might be S_1, "go downtown and buy a suit." The outcome associated with this strategy might be, C_1, "own a blue suit at a cost of $50." But if the act of going downtown is distasteful, then C_1 might be defined "own a blue suit at a cost of $50 after an uncomfortable 45-minute ride." An outcome is so inclusively defined because we wish to compare possible outcomes and choose a strategy solely on the basis of these outcomes.

Whenever it is known in advance that every strategy will lead to an unequivocal outcome we say we are in a *state of certainty*. Conceptually, decisions under certainty are the easiest to cope with: choose that strategy which leads to your most desirable outcome. We shall examine in some detail the decision situation under certainty because it will lay the foundation for the more interesting and relevant case of uncertainty.

rational decision makers

Much economic theory is concerned with states of certainty. Almost all of this theory is dominated by a "rational" man whose actions spring from the introspective question, "How shall I behave in these circumstances?" It is not always clear whether economic theories describe actual behavior or whether they attempt to prescribe behavior. The desire to advise a decision maker how he *should* behave, does not guarantee that what follows is descriptive of anybody's behavior. We are only concerned with the rational decision maker; it is essential that we define this creature carefully. An individual who does not know his own tastes and preferences is beyond our help. He should come to us only after some combination of eugenic, parental, and societal influence has instilled in him distinct preferences that are "consistent." Specifically, for a rational individual, the following axioms are valid.

AXIOM 1. When faced with any two possible outcomes, C_i and C_j, rational man will prefer C_i at least as much as C_j, and/or C_j at least as much as C_i. (If C_i is preferred at least as much as C_j, we write $C_i \geq C_j$. If $C_i \geq C_j$ and simultaneously $C_j \geq C_i$, we write $C_i = C_j$.)

AXIOM 2. If C_i is preferred at least as much as C_j and C_j is preferred at least as much as C_k, then C_i is preferred at least as much as C_k, where C_i, C_j, and C_k are any three possible outcomes. (In the above notation: If $C_i \geq C_j$ and $C_j \geq C_k$, then $C_i \geq C_k$.)

We are not claiming that rational individuals exist, but perhaps we should dispel the fear that we may be embarking upon an enterprise that will have no earthly usefulness. Surely some decision situations exist in which these two axioms describe the vast majority of us. For example, consider outcomes that involve only sums of money ranging from $1 to $100 in increments of $.01.

There are 10,000 different outcomes in this set, but for most of us their ranking is straightforward and obeys the axioms. In many situations, of course, where outcomes include many diverse dimensions, the axioms might be questioned. For example, Axiom 1 seems to be violated very often when a woman is shopping—her hesitation suggests that she may not know whether she prefers the green hat to the feathered hat. And there is much evidence that Axiom 2 is often violated, especially when the outcomes are not of very great concern to the decision maker. Nevertheless, many decision situations probably exist in which the two axioms are valid. It is these situations that will concern us in this book.

a consumer's decision problem

Consider the decision situation facing a housewife in a supermarket. The strategies available to her are staggering: the purchase of every possible combination of food items that fall within her total food budget. For instance, S_1 might be "buy 100 quarts of milk" and C_1, "family consumes 100 quarts of milk (in given time period)." Hers is the classic problem of consumer choice under certainty.[1] Without any loss in generality, we can consider the somewhat simpler situation facing her husband who is contemplating the purchase of only steak and potatoes for a barbecue.

In addition to the rationality axioms, economists assume that, within a relatively wide range, the consumer would prefer more of a good to less of a good. (If he preferred less of a good, we might then call it a *bad* rather than a *good*.) For simplicity, we will make that assumption here. We wish to advise the consumer how

[1] There is an implicit assumption that the housewife knows what she is buying. If there is some doubt because of misleading advertising, then there may be more than one possible outcome associated with each purchase. This would no longer be a problem of choice under conditions of certainty.

many pounds of steak and potatoes to buy. Let us first depict his preferences graphically. In Fig. 2-1 we measure pounds of steak

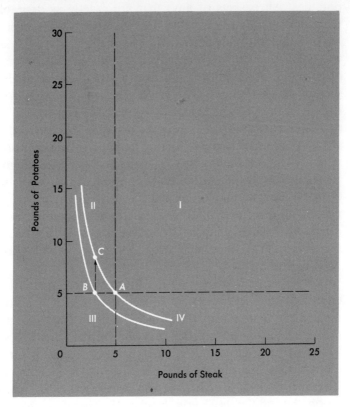

FIG. 2-1

on the horizontal axis and pounds of potatoes on the vertical axis. Every point in this quadrant represents some food basket of steak and potatoes. The point A, for example, represents the basket containing 5 pounds each of potatoes and steak. If we draw a vertical line and a horizontal line through this point, we have divided all possible food baskets into four regions. Region I, northeast of A, represents food baskets preferred to A because these baskets contain more of both steak and potatoes. Region III to the southwest of A represents food baskets that are not preferred to A since these baskets contain less of both steak and potatoes. All baskets (if any) that are exactly as desirable as A therefore lie in regions II or IV. We wish to discover all the baskets that this consumer believes equally as desirable as A. If we start with a basket containing 3 pounds of steak and 5 pounds of potatoes (point B), we know it is not preferred to A. But if we start adding potatoes to this basket (moving vertically from B in Fig. 2-1), it is conceivable that we will reach a basket that this consumer considers just as good as A. Say this happens when there are $8\frac{1}{3}$ pounds of potatoes in this basket containing 3 pounds of steak—point C. In this way, starting with different amounts of steak, we can find those amounts of potatoes that must be added to make the combination as equally attractive as basket A. Connecting all these points, we call the resulting curve an *indifference curve*. All baskets lying on this curve are equally attractive. We know the curve must slope downward (because it must lie in regions II and IV).

Proceeding in this way, we can fill the entire quadrant with indifference curves, a complete collection of which is called *a consumer's indifference map*. (See Fig. 2-3.) These curves cannot intersect as in Fig. 2-2, for if they did our axioms would be violated. This can be seen by noting that baskets A and B are equally desirable (in Fig. 2-2) because they lie on the indifference curve labeled I. Baskets A and C are also equally desirable because they lie on the indifference curve labeled II. Therefore, by Axiom 2, B and C are equally desirable. But C lies to the northeast of B and hence is preferable to B. Therefore, if our axioms and assumptions are not to lead to contradictions, a rational man's indifference curves will not intersect.

We have yet to advise our by-now-impatient consumer which basket to purchase. To do so, we must take into account his available resources. If he were not restrained, he would merely choose that basket with as much steak and potatoes as he could use. But existing prices and the funds he has limit the strategies available

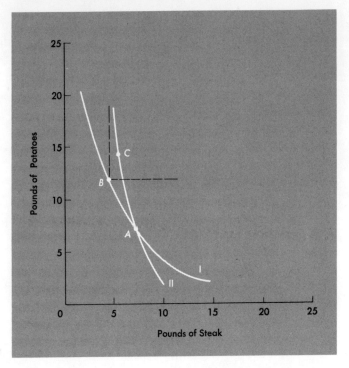

FIG. 2-2

to him. Suppose that steak costs $1.50 per pound, potatoes $.50 per pound, and our consumer wishes to spend $15. He could purchase the basket containing 10 pounds of steak and no potatoes, denoted by A in Fig. 2-3. Or he could purchase the basket containing 30 pounds of potatoes and no steak, denoted by B. In fact, his $15 will purchase any of the baskets represented by points on the line connecting A and B. This line, called the *budget line*, is determined by the prices of steak and potatoes and by the consumer's resources. This line represents all the available strategies. We would advise our man to choose that strategy which resulted in his most preferred outcome, that is, that strategy which places him on the highest possible indifference curve, because higher curves mean greater preference.

His indifference map is as shown in Fig. 2-3 (the most preferred

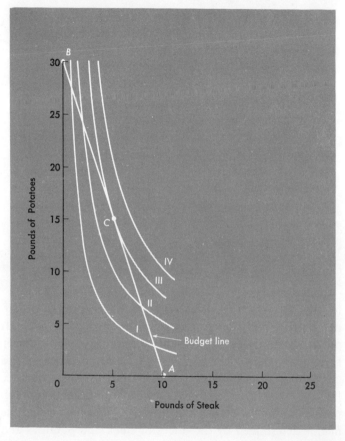

basket represented by C) where his budget line is tangent to an indifference curve. As the consumer moves down his budget line from B toward C, he is moving onto higher indifference curves. At C he reaches the highest possible curve. As he moves further

FIG. 2-3

downward toward A, he is moving onto lower indifference curves. (Economists usually assume that indifference curves are convex, or curl outward and upward from the origin. This assumption is based on observed behavior. If instead, these curves were concave, then the solution to a decision problem would involve the purchase of only one of the goods involved. Since in most situations it is observed that consumers do not specialize in the purchase of one *good*, it is then assumed that the indifference curves are convex.)

Let us review our procedure. We asked a decision maker to reveal his preferences or indifference map and the strategies available to him, that is, the size of his budget. Then we advised him to choose the basket he preferred most. In general, our advice under conditions of certainty will always be the same: choose that strategy which has the most preferred outcome. Under these circumstances, why retain an adviser?

There might be some value to the decision maker in this procedure. Which basket should he choose if the prices of the goods change, or if his budget changes? Once his preference pattern is known, these questions can be answered quickly and he need not expend energy comparing the available alternatives. There are many computational devices that will yield the correct answer— the geometrical technique we just used and some algebraic processes, notably the use of Lagrangian multipliers. (See Ref. 2.) So decision making under certainty is not a completely vacuous affair. However, the real purpose of our close scrutiny is the help it will give us in advising decision makers when the outcome for a strategy is not known with certainty.

utility functions

Suppose that outcome A is preferred at least as much as outcome B. If, in addition, outcome B is preferred at least as much as outcome A, we say that A and B are *equivalent*. All of the outcomes that are equivalent to A comprise an *equivalence class*. For example, all the outcomes represented by an indifference curve (in Fig. 2-3, say) are equivalent, and each indifference curve represents an equivalence class. The indifference map partitions all of the outcomes in a given situation into equivalence classes. If an outcome in equivalence class II is preferred to an outcome in equivalence class I, then every outcome in class II is preferred to every outcome in class I. In this case, we say that equivalence class II is preferred to equivalence class I. For example, in Fig. 2-3, the equivalence class represented by the indifference curve labeled II is preferred to the equivalence class represented by the indifference curve labeled I.

If we assign real numbers to each equivalence class so that the more preferred the equivalence class the higher the number, the assignment is called one of the decision maker's *utility functions*. A utility function is then a rule that associates with each outcome a real number so that if C_1 is preferred to C_2, then the number assigned to C_1 is greater than the number assigned to C_2. For example, a utility function might assign the numbers 5, 6, and 7 to indifference curves I, II, and III, respectively, in Fig. 2-3. Another utility function, expressing exactly the same decision maker's preferences might assign the numbers 24, 34.56, and 678 to these curves. Only the *order* of the numbers is relevant in defining these functions which are called *ordinal utility functions*.

Axioms 1 and 2 assure us that a utility function exists under most general conditions.[2] If this function can be expressed neatly, then the solution to a decision problem can be solved with little effort, no matter how the restraints operating on preferences change. For example, after plotting some points of indifference, the consumer in the barbecue example above, might have found that his preferences could be summarized in the following way: to a basket containing x pounds of steak and y pounds of potatoes, assign the number x times y. This number might then express his

[2] We could assume a third axiom involving certain topological considerations that would insure the existence of a utility function under all conditions. Because the exceptions are somewhat pathological it would be unrewarding to include such an axiom at this level of treatment. For a rigorous statement on the existence of a utility function see Gerard Debreu, "Representation of a Preference Ordering by a Numerical Function," *Decision Processes*, R. M. Thrall, C. H. Coombs, and R. L. Davis, eds., (New York: John Wiley & Sons, Inc., 1954), pp. 159–65.

preference for a basket relative to other baskets. If one basket had the number 25 assigned and another the number 9, then the basket with the higher number is preferred. The number attached to each basket is called the *utility* of the basket. It is important to realize that the utility of an outcome is a consequence of the decision maker's preference. It is merely a shorthand method of describing his preference.

In Fig. 2-1, the indifference curves could be described by the utility function which assigns to each basket the product of the number of pounds of steak by the number of pounds of potatoes. For example, the utility for point A representing 5 pounds each of potatoes and steak is 5 times 5, or 25. Note that point C also has utility 25. This utility function would be written $U(x, y) = xy$.[3] The indifference curve passing through point A could thus be labeled 25. The curve passing through point B in Fig. 2-1, could be labeled 15. Given this definition of utility, our advice to the decision maker can be summarized: Maximize your utility! This becomes a simple engineering problem if his utility function can be expressed mathematically. Herein lies the power and usefulness of the procedure outlined in this chapter. Maximizing techniques under constraints are well developed; some maximization methods use Lagrangian multipliers and linear and nonlinear programming. As a simple example let us solve the decision problem of Fig. 2-3 analytically.

an example of utility maximization

Since we know the x-axis intercept of the budget line equals 30 and its slope equals -3, the equation of the budget line in Fig. 2-3 is

(1) $y = 30 - 3x$

---

[3] In this case, since each outcome contains two goods, the utility function is a real-valued function of two variables.

where y is pounds of potatoes and x is pounds of steak. We also know the solution occurs at the point of tangency between an indifference curve and this budget line. The equation of any indifference curve may be written

(2) $xy = \text{constant} = C$

or

$$y = C/x$$

where C is the real number assigned by the utility function to each equivalence class, or indifference curve. Differentiating this for the slope of the curve yields $-C/x^2$. The solution occurs at the point where this slope is equal to the slope of the budget line

$$-C/x^2 = -3, \text{ so that } C = 3x^2$$

Substituting in (2) yields $y = 3x$ at the point of tangency. Substituting this into (1) yields

$$3x = 30 - 3x, \text{ or } x = 5$$

Again substituting into (1) we have that $y = 15$. This consumer's optimal strategy is to purchase 5 pounds of steak and 15 pounds of potatoes. This is his most preferred outcome from all the available alternatives. His utility will be $5 \times 15 = 75$.

Had we used any other utility function that maintained the same preference ordering, that is a utility function that assigned any other numbers to the curves provided that higher curves had higher numbers, this analysis would have resulted in the same solution. For example, the same preferences could be summarized by the utility function that assigns to each basket the utility $2xy$, or $U(x, y) = 2xy$.[4] This utility function would assign numbers twice as large as the original function considered in the above

[4] Any monotonic increasing function of U is again a utility function.

example, but would be maximized by the choice of the same basket.

more decision making under certainty

Another example of decision making under certainty is the so-called diet problem. Suppose the foods available to a housewife are designated by x_1, x_2, etc., and that she is concerned with the amounts of nutrients, a, b, c, . . . , that any basket of food will yield. Every basket can be designated by $(q_1, q_2, . . .)$ where q_i is the amount of x_i in the basket. If a_1 is the amount of nutrient a in a unit of x_1, a_2 the amount of nutrient a in a unit of x_2, etc. then the amount of a in a particular basket is

$$a_1 q_1 + a_2 q_2 + . . . + a_n q_n$$

The amount of b in this basket would be a similar expression with b_i's replacing the a_i's. It is sometimes said that there is a diet which meets minimum nutritional requirements measured in terms of the nutrients a, b, c, ... Suppose a housewife wishes to meet this minimal requirement at least cost. If a unit of x_i costs p_i, then the cost of any basket is

(3) $$p_1 q_1 + p_2 q_2 + . . . + p_n q_n$$

Her problem, then, is to find the least expensive basket satisfying the minimal diet requirements, that is to minimize (3) subject to inequalities of the form

$$a_1 q_1 + a_2 q_2 + . . . + a_n q_n \geq a$$
$$b_1 q_2 + b_2 q_2 + . . . + b_n q_n \geq b$$
$$\vdots$$

The technique of linear programming can be used to find a solution. In cases where the expression to be minimized is nonlinear, nonlinear programming may be used.

It might be useful to look at this problem in terms of the utility analysis developed earlier. To simplify matters, consider only two nutrients, a and b, and two foods, x and y. Suppose that 1 pound of x costs \$2 and contains 4 units of a and 2 units of b, and 1 pound of y costs \$3 and contains 3 units of a and 6 units of b. A nutrition expert declares that a minimal diet should contain 12 units of a and 18 units of b. A housewife perceives the decision situation facing her in this way: to purchase that basket of x and y that supplies at least the minimal diet at minimum cost. In Fig. 2-4 different combinations of a and b are represented by points in the quadrant. Point A represents 12 units of a and 18 units of b,

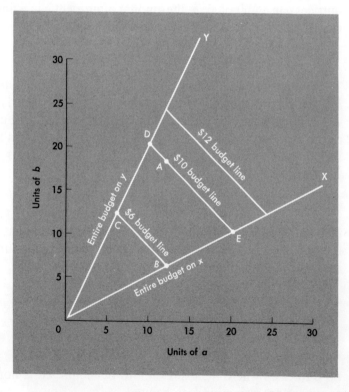

FIG. 2-4

the minimal diet. The ray from the origin marked X represents
the combinations of a and b that can be obtained solely by buying
x; the ray marked Y represents the corresponding combinations
obtained by buying y.

Again we can represent a budget line by a straight line in this
quadrant. For example, consider the ways in which $6 can be
spent on x and y. One way is to purchase 3 pounds of x, yielding
12 units of a and 6 units of b. This choice is represented by point B
in Fig. 2-4. Another way is to purchase 2 pounds of y, yielding
6 units of a and 12 units of b. This is represented by point C.
The straight line connecting B and C represents all the possible
nutritional yields arising from baskets of food containing x and y
that cost $6. Every budget line will have the same slope as this
line and will be bounded by the two lines rising from the origin.
The first step is to find the budget line that goes through A. This
is the $10 budget line; any of the points connecting D with E can
be attained for $10. For instance D can be attained by purchasing
only y and E by purchasing only x. The distance from D to A
is $\frac{1}{5}$ the distance of D to E, so to purchase the basket yielding A,
$\frac{1}{5}$ of the budget should be spent on x ($2) and $\frac{4}{5}$ on y ($8). That
is, 1 pound of x should be bought yielding 4 units of a and 2 units
of b, and $2\frac{2}{3}$ pounds of y should be bought yielding 8 units of a
and 16 units of b. This is the minimum satisfactory diet at least
cost.

Posing the problem in this way leads to an interesting preference
pattern for the decision maker. In Fig. 2-5, all baskets yielding less
than 12 units of a or 18 units of b are less preferable than A. In
addition, all baskets yielding more than 12 units of a and 18 units
of b are preferred at least as much as A. If these latter baskets are
preferred more than A, then the indifference curve passing through
A consists of the vertical line segment above A and the horizontal
line segment to the right of A. (See Fig. 2-5.) The problem can
then be stated: find the minimum cost in attaining this given level
of nutrition. (In the earlier consumer choice problem, the budget

was given and the problem was to find the highest level of preference attainable.)

This characterization of the diet problem assumes complete independence of each of the nutritional requirements. If one

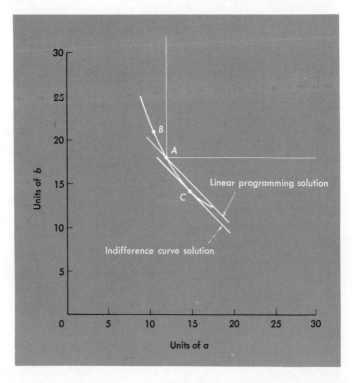

FIG. 2-5

nutrient could be substituted for another, it might be better to return to a formulation in terms of "smooth" indifference curves, instead of the sharp dog-leg of Fig. 2-4. Let us see how these alternative assumptions about utility relate to each other. Suppose that different levels of nutritional adequacy exist, and that for most relevant ranges, trades can be made between nutrient *a* and nutrient *b* without sacrificing the nutritional level. For instance, starting with A in Fig. 2-5, suppose a nutritional expert declared that if $1\frac{1}{2}$ units of a were removed from the combination and 3 units of b added, the level of nutritional adequacy would be maintained. This is represented by point B. The same level of nutrition might be described by an indifference curve similar to the one passing through A and B. The new problem might then be stated: given the level of nutrition denoted by this curve, attain it at least cost. This is now the familiar problem of finding the budget line tangent to this curve and purchasing that basket represented by the point of tangency. If substitution between nutrients is defined by smooth indifference curves, then this latter method is more efficient than the linear programming technique. The solution would now be represented by C in Fig. 2-5, which is on a lower budget line. That is, the same level of nutrition can be reached at lower cost if nutrients can be traded off against each other in some ranges.

Although this latter method is more efficient, it requires more information than the linear programming problem. It is necessary to define all the indifference curves, or levels of equal nutrition. The linear programming problem might be considered an approximation to the real problem and useful because it introduces a certain rule of thumb (the minimum diet) which renders decision making easy. When problems are very complex, introduction of rules of thumb may be justified in order to make the computations relatively easy. It is often difficult to determine how much this computational ease costs in terms of efficiency.

summary

If Axioms 1 and 2 are valid for a decision maker, we say he is *rational*. These axioms insure that he can order all possible outcomes when faced with a decision situation. If each possible strategy leads unequivocally to a single outcome, then he *should* choose that strategy which leads to his most preferred outcome. This would be trivial; but because the addition of some few assumptions to the rationality axioms leads to powerful computational techniques for solving a decision problem, this advice may be very helpful to decision makers.

Some of the devices used to select a strategy for a rational man are geometrical or algebraic, using Lagrangian multipliers or linear programming theory. *After* the decision maker reveals his preferences and constraints, these techniques can be brought into play to pinpoint the strategy he *should* follow. In this process the advisor brings no value judgments to the scene, except perhaps the criterion that the decision maker should receive his most preferred outcome.

Under most conditions, the rationality axioms insure the existence of a utility function—a rule that associates with each outcome a real number so that of any two outcomes, the more preferred has a higher number associated with it. (See Footnote 2.) If the decision maker attains a level of satisfaction measured by the utility of the outcome, then our advice can be rephrased: Maximize your utility!

PROBLEMS

1. A consumer wishes to purchase some combination of eggs and milk; the price of eggs is $1 per dozen, and the price of milk is $.50 per quart. The consumer wishes to spend $5 for this combination. His utility for a combination of X dozen eggs and y quarts of milk is X^2y. What combination of eggs and milk should he purchase?

2. In Problem 1, if his utility function is $\log(X^2y)$, what combination should he purchase?

3. Suppose a consumer preferred combination A to B whenever A contained more eggs or whenever A and B contained the same number of eggs but A had more milk. What would his indifference map look like?

REFERENCES

1. GALE, DAVID, *The Theory of Linear Economic Models*. New York: McGraw-Hill Book Company, 1960.   An excellent treatment of linear programming and the significance of solutions to economic theory.

2. HENDERSON, J. M. AND QUANDT, R. E., *Microeconomic Theory*. New York: McGraw-Hill Book Company, 1958.   Chapter 2 treats the theory of consumer choice. The Appendix contains a discussion of optimization techniques including the use of Lagrangian multipliers.

DECISION MAKING WITH OBJECTIVE PROBABILITIES

CHAPTER THREE

Man rarely inhabits the land of complete certainty. And perhaps it is a good thing. Although he seems intolerant of extreme insecurity—as evidenced by his concern for religion, science, labor unions, unemployment insurance, cartels, price fixing—it would be a dull existence if he knew with certainty the consequence of every act. Carried too far, security squeezes out many of the pleasant surprises and joys of anticipation. But we need not fret. Man may never achieve the ability to predict perfectly.

objective probabilities

Let us take one step toward reality by considering the following decision situation: each available strategy has one *or more* possible outcomes and the probability of each outcome is known. Gambling provides many examples. The toss of a coin can result in two possible outcomes, heads or tails. For most coins, and under most circumstances, we are willing to assume that the probability of either outcome is equal. This is expressed by the statement: the probability of heads is $\frac{1}{2}$ and the probability of tails is $\frac{1}{2}$. This assignment of numbers (between 0 and 1) to possible outcomes may be based upon a physical examination of the coin, or upon observing repeated tosses, or both. One interpretation of this probability statement is that if the coin is repeatedly tossed, the proportion of heads (or tails) in the total number of tosses will approach $\frac{1}{2}$. Under this interpretation, outcomes have probabilities in much the same way that physical objects have certain characteristics. We hypothesize that this book has some specific weight. Careful testing with equipment might lead us to state that the weight is 9.3 ounces. But no amount of examination can lead us to say that the weight is *exactly* 9.3 ounces, because we have no instruments that can differentiate between 9.29999999999999 and 9.3 ounces. Similarly, examination of a coin and the conditions under which it is tossed may lead us to say that the probability of heads is $\frac{1}{2}$, but we can never be sure that it is *exactly* $\frac{1}{2}$; this would require an infinite number of tosses.

In the case where many observers would be led to attach probability of $\frac{1}{2}$, or some number very close to $\frac{1}{2}$, to the outcome "heads," we say that the probability is *objective*. Objective probabilities, like physical weights do not entirely remove human judgment. Two reasonable men, with exactly the same evidence might arrive at different probabilities for "heads." But in the case of a coin these differences will usually be very small. Let us overlook the differences and assume in this chapter that reasonable men will arrive at the same probabilities in a given decision situation; we call this decision making with *objective probabilities.*

the decision situation

Again we denote strategies by $S_1, S_2, \ldots,$ and outcomes by $C_1, C_2, \ldots$. In addition, we must indicate the probability of each outcome. This can be represented conveniently in matrix form. The columns of the matrix refer to outcomes, the rows to strategies, and the entries in the body of the matrix to the objective probabilities. For example, the following matrix characterizes a decision situation with 3 available strategies and 4 possible outcomes. If S_1 is chosen, C_2 will occur with certainty; the probability of C_2 is 1 and the probability of all other outcomes is 0. The entry in the first row (referring to S_1) and the second column (referring to C_2) is 1. All other entries in the first row are 0. If S_2 is chosen, each outcome has probability $\frac{1}{4}$. For S_3, C_1 will result with probability $\frac{1}{8}$, C_2 with probability $\frac{1}{2}$, C_3 with probability $\frac{1}{4}$, and C_4 with probability $\frac{1}{8}$. Note that the probabilities in every row sum to 1, indicating that these 4 outcomes exhaust all possibilities for each strategy.

MATRIX 2.1: *Objective Probabilities for a Given Decision Situation.*

		Possible outcomes			
		C_1	C_2	C_3	C_4
	S_1	0	1	0	0
Available strategies	S_2	$\frac{1}{4}$	$\frac{1}{4}$	$\frac{1}{4}$	$\frac{1}{4}$
	S_3	$\frac{1}{8}$	$\frac{1}{2}$	$\frac{1}{4}$	$\frac{1}{8}$

This matrix of objective probabilities can be interpreted: after some strategy (say S_2) is chosen, a chance mechanism (say a roulette wheel with only 4 numbers) determines the outcome; if S_2 is chosen repeatedly, the chance mechanism will select each outcome about $\frac{1}{4}$ of the time.

expected value of a strategy

Suppose an individual had to choose between S_1 and S_2 represented in the following matrix. Choosing S_1 means playing the game where a coin is tossed and the individual wins $5 if a head appears and he loses $4 if a tail appears; and S_2 is choosing not to play.

MATRIX 2.2: *Coin Toss Game.*

	$C_1 =$ win $5	$C_2 =$ lose $4	$C_3 =$ no gain or loss
Play the game = S_1	$\frac{1}{2}$	$\frac{1}{2}$	0
Don't play = S_2	0	0	1

One way to evaluate these strategies is to calculate what would happen if either of them were chosen repeatedly. If S_2 were always chosen when the situation presented itself, the cumulative outcome, of course, would be that the decision maker would experience neither a gain nor a loss, for the outcome at every play would be 0. If S_1 were always chosen, after a large number of plays the associated probabilities indicate that about $\frac{1}{2}$ of the time a gain of $5 would result and the other half a loss of $4. For example, if S_1 were chosen 100 times, in about 50 cases a gain of $5 would result for a cumulative gain of $250, and in the remaining cases a loss of $4 would result for a cumulative loss of $200. After 100 plays, this would result in a net gain of about $50, or an average gain per play of $.50. The larger the number of plays, the closer will the average gain per play be to $.50. The average long run experience of a strategy is called the *mathematical expectation of the strategy*, or the *expected value of the strategy*. This is calculated by multiplying each outcome by its associated probability and adding all the resultant products. For example, the expected value of S_1 is $\frac{1}{2}(5) + \frac{1}{2}(-4)$, or $2.5 - 2 = 0.5$. This is written:

$$E(S_1) = 0.5$$

Since expected value represents the average result over a long period of play, it once seemed reasonable that strategies should be ranked on the basis of this calculation; that strategy with highest expected value should be chosen. This criterion would choose S_1 over S_2 in the above example. But there are individuals, even some who are not innocent of probability theory, who would not play the game; they would choose S_2. Before they are condemned, let us look at an example where the criterion of expected value breaks down completely.

the petersburg paradox

Almost from the start it was recognized that the criterion of expected value would lead to bizarre choices in some circumstances. Consider the Petersburg game. The rules are simple: a coin is repeatedly tossed and the game ends with the appearance of a head. If a head appears on the first toss and the game ends, you win \$2; if the game ends on the second toss, you win $\$2^2 = \$4$; if the game ends on the nth toss, you win $\$2^n$. Suppose the fee to play this game is your entire wealth. You are offered the chance to play (call this strategy S_1) or not to play (call this S_2). The expected value of S_2 is, of course, 0.

To calculate the expected value of S_1 we must know the probabilities of each possible outcome. Assuming a fair coin, the probability that the game will end on the first toss is $\frac{1}{2}$; the probability of it ending on the second toss is $\frac{1}{2}\frac{1}{2} = \frac{1}{4}$; the probability of it ending on the third toss is $\frac{1}{2}\frac{1}{2}\frac{1}{2} = \frac{1}{8}$; the probability of it ending on the nth toss is $(\frac{1}{2})^n$. If we multiply these probabilities with their respective outcomes (payoffs) and add, we have,

$$\tfrac{1}{2}(2) + \tfrac{1}{4}(4) + \tfrac{1}{8}(8) + \ldots + 1/n(n) + \ldots = 1 + 1 + 1 + \ldots$$

The expected value of S_1 is thus this infinite sum less your total wealth. If you apply the criterion of expected value, you would choose S_1 over S_2; you would risk your total wealth (less \$2) and play the game. If a head appeared on the first toss, your total wealth would be reduced to $2. This is contrary to what most individuals would do (except perhaps for those whose total wealth is very tiny) so the criterion of expected value is suspect. Essentially, expected value ignores the *risk* of a strategy.

For instance, if one strategy promised either $10 or $20, each with probability $\frac{1}{2}$, its expected value would be $15. But a strategy promising a *loss* of $100 or a gain of $130, each with probability of $\frac{1}{2}$, would also have an expected value of $15. Applying the criterion of expected value, an individual would be indifferent as to preference between these two strategies. Most individuals, however, would have definite preferences between them even though the two have equal expectations. Those who prefer the first might be called risk averters; those who prefer the second, risk lovers. In a world where individual preferences are free to be expressed, it is improper to call either risk averters or risk lovers wrong or irrational. We need a more subtle criterion that will allow individual attitudes toward risk to enter into the decision. The next section provides this criterion.

normative decisions with objective probabilities

The general situation involving objective probabilities can be described by the following matrix. (We do not lose much

MATRIX 2.3: *General Decision Situation.*

Basic outcomes or consequences

		C_1	C_2	$\ldots$	C_n
Available strategies	S_1	p_{11}	p_{12}		p_{1n}
	S_2	p_{21}	p_{22}		p_{2n}
	.				
	.				
	.				
	S_r	p_{r1}	p_{r2}		p_{rn}

p_{ij} = objective probability of outcome C_j if strategy S_i is chosen in generality by assuming that there are only a finite number of basic outcomes C_1, C_2, . . . , C_n. Note that in this matrix the number of available strategies may be infinite.)

Again we will define a "rational" man as one who adheres to a few assumptions or axioms. We introduce 4 axioms from which we can deduce an algorithm for ranking strategies.

AXIOM 1.   The individual has distinct and consistent preferences, that is, for any two strategies, S_i and S_j, either S_i is preferred to S_j, or vice-versa, or both. (If each is preferred to the other we again say that they are equivalent, or that S_i is indifferent to S_j and we write $S_i = S_j$.) Further, if $S_i \geq S_j$, and $S_j \geq S_k$, then $S_i \geq S_k$.

A strategy may be denoted as a vector

$$S_j = (p_{j1}C_1, p_{j2}C_2, \ldots, p_{jn}C_n)$$

We distinguish n strategies (which may or may not actually be available to the decision maker) in which all the objective probabilities are 0 except for the one which is 1. These are the *pure* strategies that correspond to complete certainty. For example, $S_i^* = (0C_1, 0C_2, \ldots, 1C_i, \ldots, 0C_n)$. Since S_i^* leads unequivocally to C_i as the outcome, we can replace C_i whenever it occurs in an expression by S_i^*. That is, we can identify any outcome with that pure strategy which will result in that outcome with certainty.

If Axiom 1 is valid, we can rank all the pure strategies. Since the numbering of strategies is arbitrary, let S_1^* be the most preferred among the pure strategies, S_2^* the second most preferred, etc., with S_n^* the least preferred. This numbering of course automatically ranks the basic outcomes: $C_1 \geq C_2 \ldots \geq C_n$.

If only pure strategies are available in a given context, then the decision problem is reduced to one of complete certainty of the kind that has been explored in Chap. 2. Obviously, if S_1^* actually appears among the available strategies, it will be the most preferred.

AXIOM 2.   Every pure strategy is equivalent to a unique mixed strategy involving only C_1 and C_n, that is, for every S_i^* there exists a unique probability u_i so that $S_i^* = (u_iC_1, 0C_2, 0C_3, \ldots, [1 - u_i]C_n)$. (This last strategy can be written $[u_iC_1, (1 - u_i)C_n]$, it being understood that when any of the objective probabilities is 0, that term will not appear in the vector.) The decision maker will be indifferent as to choice between the pure strategy S_i^* and the mixed strategy whose outcomes are C_1 with probability u_i and C_n with probability $(1 - u_i)$. The probability u_i is called the *utility* of C_i.

Since this axiom is crucial to the development that follows, it will be illustrated with an example. Suppose C_1 represents a gain of $100, C_2 a gain of $99, \ldots, C_{100}$ a gain of $1. This would be a decision situation in which the basic outcomes are gains ranging from $1 to $100, with higher gains preferred to lesser gains. S_{76}^* is the pure strategy promising $25 with complete certainty. Let $S_p = [p \ \$100, (1 - p) \ \$1]$ be any strategy involving only the best and worst outcomes. From axiom 1 we know that S_{76}^* and S_p can be compared. If, for example, $p = 0.01$, so that S_p represents the strategy that will result in a gain of $100 with 0.01 probability and $1 with 0.99 probability, most individuals would probably prefer S_{76}^*. That is, most would prefer $25 with certainty rather than a small chance at winning $100 and a large chance of winning $1. (What is the expectation of S_p?) Now if p is continuously increased, Axiom 2 states that some probability will be reached at which S_p is indifferent to S_{76}^*; and if this point is exceeded, then S_p will be preferred to S_{76}^*. For example, if $p = 0.99$, most would probably prefer S_p over the certainty of $25, since S_p now promises $100 with a very large probability.

Suppose when $p = 0.5$, a decision maker is indifferent as to choice between S_p and S_{76}^*, that is, a decision maker is indifferent between receiving $25 with certainty and a strategy that will return either $100 or $1, both with probability $\frac{1}{2}$. (In our notation, $S_{76}^* = (\frac{1}{2} \cdot 100, \frac{1}{2} \cdot 1) = [u_{76} \cdot 100, (1 - u_{76}) \cdot 1]$.) Then the probability $u_{76} = \frac{1}{2}$ is called the utility of $25. Note that this probability, or utility, does not refer to the uncertainty introduced by nature but to the preferences of the decision maker.

Axiom 2 implies delicate discriminatory powers on the part of the decision maker. Except where the basic outcomes lend themselves to easy discrimination, such as when the basic outcomes involve sums of money, it is sometimes said this axiom is unrealistic and may not be true.

AXIOM 3. In any strategy, the component strategy C_i can be replaced by its equivalent strategy involving only C_1 and C_n.

Recall that the pure strategy C_i can be replaced by S_i^*, which is equivalent to a unique mixed strategy $[u_iC_1, (1 - u_i)C_n]$. Axiom 3 asserts that this last strategy can replace C_i in *any* strategy. For example, consider an arbitrary strategy, $S = (p_1C_1, p_2C_2, \ldots, p_nC_n)$. If we replace each C_i with its equivalent mixed strategy, we have

$$S = \{p_1[u_1C_1, (1 - u_1)C_n], p_2[u_2C_1, (1 - u_2)C_n], \ldots, \\ p_n[u_nC_1, (1 - u_n)C_n]\}$$

The strategy S which is called a *compound mixed strategy, or simply a compound strategy,* since each "outcome" C_i can itself be represented as a mixed strategy which then leads to one of the basic outcomes C_1 or C_n. Intuitively, this axiom is reasonable if only the basic outcomes are relevant to the decision maker; the manner in which a basic outcome is attained has no bearing on the decision maker's preference. In Chap. 2 we defined the basic outcomes so that they incorporated all the relevant aspects of interest to the individual. If this can always be done, then this axiom is plausible. If, however, the strategy itself carries some degree of satisfaction not apparent in the outcome, then the decision situation will violate this axiom. In other words, this axiom applies to situations where it does not matter how you play the game, it is what you win that counts.

A numerical example may make the replacement process clear. Let $S = [\frac{1}{4} (\$10), \frac{1}{2} (\$40), \frac{1}{4} (\$80)]$. Suppose that the component strategy promising \$10 with certainty is equivalent to the basic mixed strategy $[0.3 (\$100), 0.7 (\$1)]$, \$40 is equivalent to the basic mixed strategy $[0.7 (\$100), 0.3 (\$1)]$, and \$80 is equivalent to

[0.9 ($100), 0.1 ($1)]. Substituting these equivalent strategies in S yields:

$\{\frac{1}{4}[0.3\ (\$100),\ 0.7\ (\$1)],\ \frac{1}{2}[0.7\ (\$100),\ 0.3\ (\$1)],\ \frac{1}{4}[0.9\ (\$100),\ 0.1\ (\$1)]\}$

We have replaced each basic outcome ($10, $40, and $80) with a mixed strategy that promises a return of either $100 or $1. The resulting reduced strategy therefore involves, after a two-step derivation, only the two basic outcomes $100 and $1. The compound strategy results in either the best or worst outcome after two steps: first, a chance mechanism determines whether the first, second, or third equivalent reduced strategies is chosen; second, another chance mechanism determines whether the best or worst outcome results. The first equivalent reduced strategy will be chosen with probability $\frac{1}{4}$, the second with probability $\frac{1}{2}$, and the third with probability $\frac{1}{4}$. The following diagram illustrates this compound strategy.

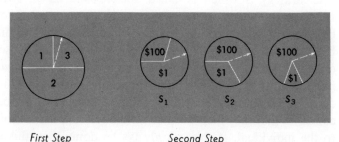

First Step

Spin pointer, if it
stops in region 1,
choose S_1; if in 2,
S_2; if in 3, S_3

Second Step

Spin pointer of appropriate wheel
to determine whether $100 or $1
results

Since either the best or worst outcome will result after two steps suggests that any compound strategy can be reduced to a basic mixed strategy that is a lottery involving only the best and worst outcomes. For instance, note in the diagram above that if the compound strategy is chosen a large number of times, in the first step, wheel S_1 will be chosen about $\frac{1}{4}$ of the time; and in these cases, \$100 will result about 30 per cent of the time; that is, \$100 will result $\frac{1}{4}$ (30 per cent) of the time, or $7\frac{1}{2}$ per cent of the time. In the first step, wheel S_2 will be chosen $\frac{1}{2}$ of the time; and in these cases, \$100 will result 70 per cent of the time; that is, \$100 will result $\frac{1}{2}$ (70 per cent) of the time or 35 per cent of the time. Also in the first step, the wheel S_3 will be chosen $\frac{1}{4}$ of the time; and in these cases \$100 will result 90 per cent of the time; that is, \$100 will result $\frac{1}{4}$ (90 per cent) of the time or $22\frac{1}{2}$ per cent of the time. Combining all the possible ways in which \$100 will be the final result, we see that after a large number of plays, \$100 will be the final basic outcome $7\frac{1}{2} + 35 + 22\frac{1}{2}$, or 65 per cent of the time. Since we are assuming that it is only the final outcomes that concern the individual, these substitutions and reductions indicate that the original compound strategy is equivalent to the reduced compound strategy [0.65.(\$100), 0.35 (\$1)].

In summary, we started with an arbitrary strategy S, converted it into a compound strategy which in turn was reduced to a basic mixed strategy involving only the best and worst outcomes. S, the compound strategy, and the resulting simple strategy were all equivalent.

In general, if $(p_1C_1, \ldots, pC_n)$ is any strategy, it will be equivalent to a basic mixed strategy $(qC_1, (1 - q)C_n)$ where $q = p_1u_1 + p_2u_2 + \ldots + p_nu_n$, and u_i is the utility of C_i.

AXIOM 4.   If any two strategies involve only the best and worst outcomes, that strategy which places the highest probability on the best outcome will be preferred. For example, if S = [0.8 (\$100), 0.2 (\$1)] and S' = [0.7 (\$100), 0.3 (\$1)], then a rational individual would prefer S over S'.

These four axioms allow our rational man to compare two complex strategies by reducing them to basic mixed strategies of the form of Axiom 3 and then choosing the strategy that makes C_1 more probable. When a complex strategy is reduced to a basic mixed strategy involving only C_1 and C_n, the probability associated with C_1 is

$$p = p_1u_1 + p_2u_2 + \ldots + p_nu_n,$$

where p_i is the probability of C_i in the complex strategy and u_i is the utility of C_i. In a statistical sense, p is the "average" utility of the complex strategy; if this strategy is followed repeatedly u_i will occur with a frequency indicated by the probability p_i, and the average utility experienced will be p. The larger p, the more preferred the strategy. Note the resemblance between the expression defining p and the expression for expected value discussed earlier. If we replace each u_i by C_i, we have the mathematical expectation, or expected value of the strategy. We noted that this procedure did not permit us to rank strategies. The four axioms have allowed us to replace each C_i (an objective measure) with a u_i (a subjective measure that will vary from individual to individual), then the strategies were ranked on the basis of *expected utility*, rather than expected value.

To summarize results so far—if an individual has consistent preferences among all possible strategies in a given situation, then he can associate with each basic outcome a number we call its utility, so that if he prefers C_i to C_j then $u_i \geq u_j$. Furthermore, he will prefer a strategy S_i over S_j if the expected utility of S_i is greater than the expected utility of S_j.

cardinal versus ordinal utility

The assignment of utilities to basic outcomes is called the *individual's utility function*. The utility function places a *relative* value on each basic outcome that expresses the individual's subjective attitude toward risk. This utility function, like the utility function for basic outcomes under complete certainty derived in Chap. 2 has the property that the more desirable the basic outcome, the higher the utility associated with it. But unlike the ordinal utility function for riskless situations, the utility function derived in this chapter from consistent preferences among strategies is more restricted in its nature. Recall that an ordinal utility function when transformed so that the new values maintain the same *order*, will still express the same preference pattern as the untransformed utility function. Thus, an ordinal utility function that assigns utilities 0, 0.1, 0.3, and 0.4 to C_1, C_2, C_3, and C_4, expresses exactly the same preferences, and will lead to exactly the same selection of strategy in any given situation as a utility function which assigns utilities of 1, 3, 9, and 18 to these basic outcomes.[1]

The utility function derived in this chapter does not have this *ordinal* property—the relative magnitudes of the utilities have relevance. In particular, only if each utility value is changed in a specific way, will the resulting transformed utility function express identical preferences: if each utility value is multiplied by some constant, $k > 0$, to which is added some constant, a, then the resulting utility function will lead to the same preference ranking among mixed strategies. That is, if $u' = a + ku$, then u' defines the same preference structure as u.

If we adopt the convention that $u(C_1) = 1$ and $u(C_n) = 0$, that is, we assign utility of 1 to the best outcome and 0 to the worst, then the utility function derived here is unique. This utility function, where the relative magnitudes are meaningful, is called a *cardinal utility function*. (The word "ordinal" is used to indicate that only the order property of the real numbers is used; "cardinal" is used to indicate not only the order property, but also the property of magnitude.)

In Chap. 2 we showed that an individual with consistent preferences, under complete certainty, made decisions *as if* he were maximizing an ordinal utility function. In this chapter we have shown that a rational individual (one obeying our axioms) when

---

[1] This property can be expressed mathematically: if u is an ordinal utility function, then $f(u)$ is also a utility function leading to exactly the same decisions provided that $f' > 0$.

faced with strategies involving risk, (strategies involving objective probabilities) behaves *as if* he were maximizing a cardinal utility function. It is important to note that from consistent preferences we *deduced* utility functions, not vice-versa. The utility function is merely a compact description of the individual's preferences. Because we have shown that utility functions exist for rational individuals under certain circumstances, we are able to use analytical methods for choosing the optimal strategy from a large set of available strategies without having to compare all strategies. This is the real purpose of the preceding construction. Otherwise we could be criticized for having built a complex mechanism merely to tell a decision maker that he should choose that strategy which he prefers most—gratuitous advice at best.

resolving the petersburg paradox

Historically, the notion of utility preceded the axiomatic construction presented here. Utility was interpreted as a measure of "satisfaction." In this way, Bernoulli was able to explain the Petersburg game. His hypothesis states that individuals derive greater and greater satisfaction from increasing wealth, but the *rate of increase* of satisfaction declines in proportion to the individual's wealth: a millionaire receives much less satisfaction (utility) from an additional dollar than does a pauper. The hypothesis is that individuals maximize *satisfaction*, not wealth.

It must have seemed natural to Bernoulli, at a time when many laws of the universe were discovered and expressed in mathematical form, that man's satisfaction from wealth should also be governed by some law. If there were any justice in the world, this law might be expressed with some elegant formula. One mathematical function which had the required properties was the *logarithm* of wealth. This was seized upon by Bernoulli. First, it accorded higher utilities to higher wealth; its first derivative was positive. Second, the rate of increase in satisfaction decreased with

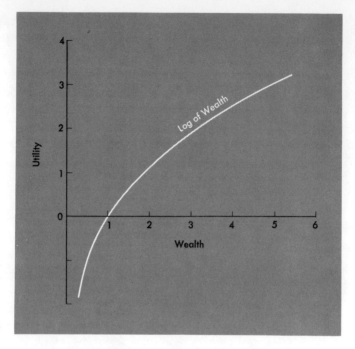

FIG. 3-1

increasing wealth; the second derivative was negative. (See Fig. 3-1.)

Now an individual offered the chance to play the Petersburg game would reach his decision by calculating his expected utility

$$\tfrac{1}{2} \log 2 + \tfrac{1}{4} \log 4 + \tfrac{1}{8} \log 8 + \ldots +$$

minus the utility of the entrance fee. This infinite series has a finite sum and so might lead to a decision to play. But unfortunately, this does not resolve the paradox. For now we can construct a game whose expected *utility* is infinite and again would lead an individual to play no matter how expensive the entrance fee. Suppose that if the game ends on the first toss, you win $\$e^2$, on the second toss $\$e^{2^2}$, on the nth toss, $\$e^{2^n}$. Using Bernoulli's utility function,[2] the utility of $\$e^2 = 2$, of $\$e^{2^2} = 4$, $\$e^{2^n} = 2^n$, so that the expected *utility* of the game is again infinite; $\frac{2}{2} + \frac{4}{4} + \frac{8}{8} + \ldots$.

A payoff scheme can always be devised which will lead to this paradox if the utility function is unbounded. Let $u(w)$ be an unbounded utility function of wealth. Now consider the inverse of u (see fig. 3-2). The inverse of u, written u^{-1}, is defined for every value of w, so that we can define the payoff at the nth toss to be:

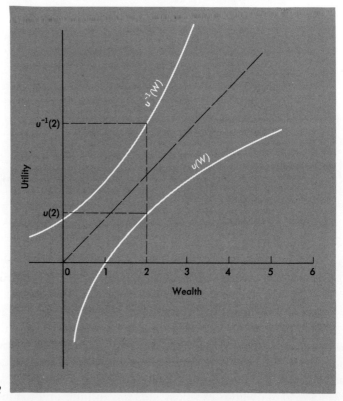

FIG. 3-2

[2] We are considering natural logarithms with base e, so that $\log(e^x) = x$.

$u^{-1}(2^n)$. Then the utility of this expression is $u[u^{-1}(2^n)] = 2^n$, leading to the troublesome infinite sum.

One escape from the paradox is to assume that the utility is always increasing but *bounded* above. Suppose we assume that utility never exceeds 1 no matter how large wealth becomes. This immediately suggests the utility function $u = 1 - \frac{1}{w}$. (See Fig. 3-3.) This gives rise to the sum

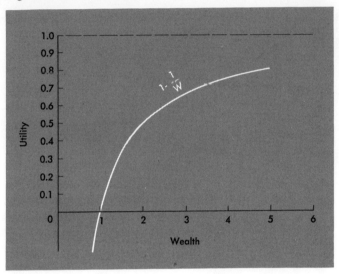

FIG. 3-3

$$\frac{1}{2} \cdot \frac{1}{2} + \frac{1}{4} \cdot \frac{3}{4} + \frac{1}{8} \cdot \frac{7}{8} + \ldots + \frac{1}{2^n} \cdot \frac{2^n - 1}{2^n} + \ldots$$

It can be shown that this infinite series sums to $\frac{2}{3}$. The expected utility of the Petersburg game is $\frac{2}{3}$. This is the utility of \$3. Therefore an individual with this utility function would not play if the entrance fee exceeded \$3. This seems to characterize an extremely cautious individual with high aversion to gambling. A less cautious individual might have a utility function of the form

$$u(w) = 1 - \frac{1}{w^z} \qquad \text{where } 0 < z < 1$$

The smaller z, the more an individual would pay.

But there is no need to search for "the" utility function of wealth. It is recognized now that risk attitudes differ substantially between individuals. One man's risk is another man's insurance against boredom.

PROBLEMS

1. A mail order firm ran an advertisement for 100 weeks for a $10 item with the following results:

NO. OF WEEKS	NO. OF ORDERS
5	100
10	120
20	180
40	200
20	210
5	280

If this pattern persists, what are the expected sales for any week?

2. Suppose in Problem 1 that the firm advertises 3 different products with prices of $20, $10, and $5. Most of the orders are for the $10 item, but 25 per cent are for the $5 item and 20 per cent for the $20 item. What are the firm's expected sales for any week?

3. You have $20,000. You are offered a ship and cargo for $10,000. If the ship arrives safely in the Orient you can sell its cargo for $12,000. If the ship then returns safely to the United States you can sell it for $8,000. ——

   a. If the probability of a safe voyage out or back is $\frac{1}{2}$, what is the expected profit of this investment?

   b. What probability would make it a "fair" bet or zero profit?

   c. If your utility for wealth is the (common) logarithm of wealth, what probability would leave you indifferent toward this investment?

   d. Calculate your own utility for each possible outcome by comparing the choice between the outcome with certainty, and some lottery involving the best and worst outcome. What probability for success of voyage would leave you indifferent toward this investment?

REFERENCES

1. FISHBURN, PETER C., *Decision and Value Theory*. New York: John Wiley & Sons, Inc., 1964.   A comprehensive treatment of decision making with probabilities. Chapter 5 contains a fine discussion of the foundations of probability.

2. LUCE, R. DUNCAN, AND RAIFFA, HOWARD, *Games and Decisions*. New York: John Wiley & Sons, Inc., 1958.   An exciting and beautiful book. Chapter 2 is an excellent discussion of cardinal utility.

3. VON NEUMANN, JOHN AND MORGENSTERN, OSKAR, *Theory of Games and Economic Behavior*. New York: John Wiley & Sons, Inc., 1964. The seminal work on game theory. Chapter 1 and the Appendix treat cardinal utility theory.

DECISION MAKING WITH SUBJECTIVE PROBABILITIES

CHAPTER FOUR

When we leave the casino or the laboratory, objective probabilities seem to disappear. Consider the statement: the probability that Jones will be elected president is 0.4. We cannot repeat the election many times to see if the number of times Jones is elected approaches the fraction $\frac{4}{10}$. It could be argued that if it were possible to hold a large number of elections under the conditions that now prevail, Jones would be elected about 40 per cent of the time. The fact that in practice we cannot carry out this experiment does not

invalidate the statement. Perhaps, but this statement is still quali-
tatively different from the statements involving objective probabilities. The essential difference is that two reasonable men weigh-
ing exactly the same information may arrive at very different
probabilities. In this chapter, we will look at situations where
objective probabilities do not exist but where an individual still
has clear-cut preferences among a set of strategies.

subjective probability

The most prevalent (and interesting) decision situations
do not involve certainty or objective probabilities. Political strategy is based on the likelihood of war and peace, and throughout
history different policy makers have held very different estimates.
In the stock market an individual who believes the likelihood of
falling prices to be greater than the likelihood of rising prices
makes a decision to sell a security to an individual whose expectations are more sanguine. Bankers and businessmen often view
quite differently the chances of success for an enterprise; bettors
at a horse race often have different "favorites."

In this chapter we show that if an individual has clear-cut,
consistent preferences over a specified set of strategies he will act
as if he assigned probabilities to various outcomes. These probabilities, called subjective probabilities, have all the mathematical
properties of objective probabilities except that they are unique
to the individual. Just as the utility function derived in Chap. 3
summarizes the individual's risk attitude by placing a relative
value on the basic outcomes, these subjective probabilities summarize the individual's intensity of belief in the possibility of
various outcomes. Again we introduce some axioms; if these
axioms are appropriate in a given situation we show that a
rational individual will make decisions by maximizing expected
utility.

the existence of subjective probabilities

Consider an individual who must choose between S_1, campaign for candidate Jones and give up present employment, and S_2, do not campaign and continue in present job. If he chooses S_1 and Jones is elected, he will be appointed to a position paying $20,000 a year; if Jones is not elected he will have to accept a position paying $10,000 a year. If he chooses S_2 he will continue to make $15,000 a year whether Jones is elected or not. His decision hinges on his utility for income and his estimate of Jones's chance for success. This decision situation can be summarized in the following matrix:

MATRIX 4.1: *Decision Situation Without Objective Probabilities.*

	W_1 = Jones elected	W_2 = Jones defeated
S_1 = campaign for Jones	Make $20,000 a year	Make $10,000 a year
S_2 = do not campaign	Make $15,000 a year	Make $15,000 a year

W_1 and W_2 are the "states of the world" that will be the result after the votes are counted. If objective probabilities can be attached to these states, this individual would then choose the strategy that maximizes his utility for income. However, if it is a typical election beset with many uncertainties (a scandal may taint one of the candidates before election; some event such as war, outside the influence of either candidate, may change the appeal of one candidate to the voters; a slip of the tongue in a campaign speech may alter a candidate's prospects dramatically; a close associate of one of the candidates may suddenly be uncovered as a felon) then reasonable men faced with the same evidence may differ widely about Jones's prospects. Nevertheless, we will show that if the individual now choosing between S_1 and S_2 has distinct and consistent preferences over a relevant set of alternatives, then his choice will be made as if he assigned a numerical quantity to W_1 (we call this quantity his subjective probability that Jones will be elected), and he will operate with this probability to maximize his utility in exactly the same fashion as the individual in Chap. 3 who operated with objective probabilities.

Let us generalize this situation by introducing s possible "states of the world," $W_1, W_2, \ldots, W_s$. Again we assume that there are n basic outcomes, $C_1, C_2, \ldots, C_n$, so that he prefers C_1 most and C_n least. Then a decision matrix can be constructed:

MATRIX 4.2: *A Generalized Decision Situation Without Objective Probabilities Involving Basic Outcomes.*

	W_1	W_2	$\ldots$	W_s
S_1	C_{11}	C_{12}	$\ldots$	C_{1s}
S_2	C_{21}	C_{22}		C_{2s}

Denote by E_i the strategy $(D_{i1}, D_{i2}, \ldots, D_{is})$, where D_{ij} is a strategy involving *objective* probabilities

$$(1) \qquad D_{ij} = (p_1C_1, p_2C_2, \ldots, p_nC_n)$$

Then we can generalize Matrix 2 even further:

MATRIX 4.3: *A Generalized Decision Situation Without Objective Probabilities Involving Risky Outcomes.*

	W_1	W_2	$\ldots$	W_s
E_1	D_{11}	D_{12}		D_{1s}
E_2	D_{21}	D_{22}		D_{2s}

For example, if E_1 is chosen in Matrix 3, then the outcome will be D_{11} if W_1 is the state of the world, D_{12} is the outcome if W_2 is the state of the world, etc. To say that D_{11} is the outcome means that this strategy involving objective probabilities will be the result; so that now a spin of some wheel will determine which basic outcome, C_i, will result. For example, if $D_{11} = (p_1C_1, p_nC_n)$, then a basic outcome is reached in two steps: first, a "true" state of the world is observed (in this case W_1) and second, outcome C_1 will result with objective probability p_1 or C_n will result with probability C_n. (D_{ij} may of course be a pure strategy that results in some C_k with certainty.)

Now, one last generalization; consider the set of all strategies of the form

(2) $(p_1E_1, p_2E_2, \ldots, p_nE_s)$

where again the p_i's represent objective probabilities. Strategies of this form culminate in a basic outcome after three steps:

> *Step 1:* Spin a wheel to select $E_i = [D_1, D_2, \ldots, D_s]$. The determination of E_i is subject to the objective probabilities of Expression (2).
>
> *Step 2:* If "true" state of world is W_j then D_j results.
>
> *Step 3:* Spin a wheel to select C_k. This determination is subject to the objective probabilities of Expression (1).

Let us call the set of all strategies of the form as in Matrix 4.3 A^*, and the set of all strategies of the form of expression (2) R^*. We can now exploit the axiomatic structure of Chap. 3 if we identify A^* with the set of basic outcomes, $A = (C_1, C_2, \ldots, C_n)$ and R^* with the set of all possible strategies involving objective probabilities and basic outcomes, i.e., with the set R whose elements appear as $(p_1C_1, p_2C_2, \ldots, p_nC_n)$. These constructs are set forth in the following table.

Now if the axioms of Chap. 3 apply for R^*, that is, if an individual has clear-cut consistent preferences among the elements of R^*, then by precisely the same reasoning in Chap. 3, there exists a utility function over R^* which we call u^*. (It might be argued that the strategies in R^* are too complex for an individual to

OBJECTIVE PROBABILITY	SUBJECTIVE PROBABILITY
	$\{W_1, W_2, \ldots, W_s\}$ = possible states of world
$A = \{C_1, C_2, \ldots, C_n\}$ = set of basic outcomes	$A^* = \{[(D_1, D_2, \ldots, D_s)]\}$ = set of all possible strategies where D_i results if true state of world is W_i. Each D_i is an element of R.
$R = \{(p_1 C_1, p_2 C_2, \ldots, p_n C_n)\}$ = set of all possible strategies using objective probabilities. $\Downarrow$ utility function so that $u(C_i) = u_i$ and $u(p_1 C_1, \ldots, p_n C_n) = p_1 u_1 + p_2 u_2 + \cdots + p_n u_n$	$R^* = \{(p_1 E_1, \ldots, p_n E_s)\}$ = set of all strategies involving objective probabilities. Each E_i is an element of A^*. $\Downarrow$ $u^*(W_i^*) = p_i^* =$ subjective probability of state of world W_i.

compare. This is probably true when the basic outcomes are diverse in nature. However, when the basic outcomes involve different sums of money, these strategies are not far removed from the Irish Sweepstakes where a lottery determines the winners of horse race tickets, which in turn determine money prizes to winners.)

For example, consider the decision situation of Matrix 1. The set of basic outcomes consists of C_1 = make \$20,000 a year, C_2 = make \$15,000 a year, and C_3 = make \$10,000 a year. There are two possible states of the world, W_1 = Jones elected, and W_2 = Jones defeated. An element of R has the form (p_1 \$20,000, p_2 \$15,000, p_3 \$10,000); this is a strategy with objective probabilities that results in \$20,000 with probability p_1, \$15,000 with probability p_2, and \$10,000 with probability p_3. Call this strategy D_1. Another element of R with probabilities p_1', p_2', and p_3' call D_2. Now $[D_1, D_2]$ is an element of A^*; it is the strategy that results in D_1 if the true state of the world is W_1, otherwise it results in D_2. Call this element of A^*, E_1. Another element of A^* may be denoted by $[D_3, D_4] = E_2$. Now an element of R^* has the form $(p_1'' E_1, p_2'' E_2) = F_1$. Now suppose the probabilities have the following values:

$$p_1 = \tfrac{1}{4} \qquad p_1' = \tfrac{1}{2} \qquad p_1'' = \tfrac{1}{8}$$
$$p_2 = \tfrac{1}{2} \qquad p_2' = \tfrac{3}{8} \qquad p_2'' = \tfrac{3}{4}$$
$$p_3 = \tfrac{1}{4} \qquad p_3' = \tfrac{1}{8} \qquad p_3'' = \tfrac{1}{8}$$

Then F_1 is the compound strategy that looks like this

$$[\tfrac{1}{4}(D_1, D_2), \tfrac{3}{4}(D_3, D_4), \tfrac{1}{8}(D_5, D_6)] =$$
$$[\tfrac{1}{4}(\tfrac{1}{4} \cdot \$20{,}000, \tfrac{1}{2} \cdot \$15{,}000, \tfrac{1}{4} \cdot \$10{,}000),$$
$$(\tfrac{1}{2} \cdot \$20{,}000, \tfrac{3}{8} \cdot \$15{,}000, \tfrac{1}{8} \cdot \$10{,}000)], \tfrac{3}{4}(\ldots)$$

This is a very cumbersome expression, but if it does not matter to the individual whether a wheel is first spun and then the state of the world determined or vice-versa (and this is implicit in our assumption earlier that the individual is interested only in the basic outcome and not the strategy), then the expression F_1 can be reduced to the form

$$(D_1', D_2')$$

This last strategy results in a compound strategy D_1' if the true state of the world is W_1, and D_2' if otherwise. In this way, elements of R^* are not as complex as they first seem; there are probably many situations in which an individual can express clear preferences among such strategies.

Now consider those elements in R^* where some unique E_i always results from Step 1. We can then identify E_i with this element; call the utility associated with this element of R^*, $u^*(E_i)$. Again, we consider a special subset of the E_i, those of the form $E_i = [C_i, C_j, \ldots, C_k]$, i.e., strategies as depicted in Matrix 2. Let $u^*([C_1, C_1, \ldots, C_1]) = 1$ and $u^*[(C_n, C_n, \ldots, C_n)] = 0$, that is, the utility of the most preferred strategy (that which will result with certainty in the most preferred basic outcome) equals 1, and the utility of the least preferred equals 0. Then let

$$u_1^*([C_1, C_n, C_n, \ldots, C_n]) = u_1^*(W_1^*) = p_1^*$$
$$u_2^*([C_n, C_1, C_n, \ldots, C_n]) = u_2^*(W_2^*) = p_2^*$$
$$\vdots$$
$$u_i^*([C_n, \ldots, C_1, \ldots, C_n]) = u_i^*(W_i^*) = p_i^*$$

Then it can be shown (see Reference 1) that the p_i^* sum to 1 and that

$$(3) \qquad u^*(D_1, D_2, \ldots, D_s) = p_1^* u(D_1) + \ldots + p_s^* u(D_s)$$

The number p_i^* is called the subjective probability of the ith state of the world. (The numbers $u(D_i)$ are the utilities associated with the strategies involving objective probabilities.)

Note that in Expression (3) the numbers p_i^* are used in exactly the same way that objective probabilities were used in Chap. 3. This individual's preferences gave rise to the subjective probabilities of the various states of the world and the utility associated with each basic outcome, and he ranked preferences by maximizing his subjective expected utility.

summary

Essentially, the axioms of utility theory set out in Chap. 3 have been used again to derive subjective probabilities. A new set of strategies, R^*, was defined. These strategies were compound in nature and involved objective probabilities and the resultant true state of the world. In situations in which an individual can express distinct and consistent preferences over this set, we saw that his preferences could be summarized by a "utility" function, u^*, on this set. By normalizing this function, that is, setting u^* of the most preferred element equal to 1 and u^* of the least preferred equal to 0, it was shown that u^* of the element of R^* that returns the most preferred outcome C_1 if state of the world W_i results and C_n otherwise can be interpreted as the subjective probability that the true state of the world is W_i. These probabilities have all the mathematical characteristics of objective probabilities; the individual's preferences then dictate that he maximizes subjective expected utility when choosing a strategy from those available to him.

It might be worth emphasizing that the demands on the decision maker are more severe when working with subjective probabilities than when working under certainty or with objective probabilities.

PROBLEM

1. A businessman must choose from S_1, S_2, and S_3 in the following matrix. (S_4 and S_5 are not available to him.)

	Peace W_1	War W_2	Cold War W_3
S_1	100	-50	20
S_2	-50	100	20
S_3	20	20	20
S_4	100	-50	-50
S_5	-50	100	-50

The entries in the matrix represent his profit or loss. The states of the world concern our relations with Russia for the year 1972. S_1 is the strategy to build a factory in Germany; S_2 is the strategy to build a munitions plant in U.S.; S_3 is the strategy to build a bakery in U.S. The businessman's utility for money is linear and he wishes to maximize his expected profit. He claims he would be indifferent between S_4 (if it were available to him) and a simple lottery that returned a loss of 50 with probability $\frac{1}{4}$ and a gain of 100 with probability $\frac{3}{4}$. He is also indifferent between S_5 (if it were available to him) and a lottery that returned a loss of 50 with probability $\frac{7}{8}$ and a gain of 100 with probability $\frac{1}{8}$.

    a. What is the businessman's subjective probability that war will occur; that the cold war will continue; and that peace will ensue?

    b. Which strategy will he select?

    c. Determine *your* subjective probabilities for W_1, W_2, and W_3. Then determine your utility for the outcomes -50, 20, and 100. Which strategy will you select from S_1, S_2, and S_3?

REFERENCES

1. ANSCOMBE, F. J., AND AUMANN, R. J., "A Definition of Subjective Probability," *The Annals of Mathematical Statistics*, 34, (1963), 199–205.   This article is the basis for the development of subjective probabilities in this book.

2. LUCE, R. D. AND RAIFFA, H., *Games and Decisions*. New York: John Wiley & Sons, Inc., 1958.

3. RAMSEY, F. P., "Truth and Probability," *The Foundations of Mathematics*. Paterson, N.J.: Littlefield, Adams, 1960, Chap. VII. This article was first published in 1926 and is probably the first treatment of subjective probability that has culminated in Savage's development. (See next reference.)

4. SAVAGE, L. J., *The Foundations of Statistics*. New York: John Wiley & Sons, Inc., 1954.   A rigorous development of utility and subjective probability without using the concept of objective probability. Both utility and subjective expectations are derived from axioms.

5. SCHLAIFER, R., *Probability and Statistics for Business Decisions*. New York: McGraw-Hill, Inc., 1959.   Numerous applications of maximizing utility with subjective probabilities. Almost all the examples and problems are in the area of business and management.

AN APPLICATION PORTFOLIO SELECTION

CHAPTER FIVE

Maximizing utility with subjective probabilities requires delicate estimates; first the individual must know his risk attitude (his utility function for the basic outcomes), and second, he must have a finely graded estimate of the likelihood of future events. When the basic outcomes are money income (or gain) it seems reasonable that an individual will not only be able to rank the outcomes, but also to rank various lotteries involving these outcomes. If this is so, then his utility function can be determined. When the possible states of the world are also measured on one axis, such as the possible price of a stock on some date in the future, then it is conceivable that an individual can express fine judgments about the probabilities of these states.

One area of human behavior in which these conditions seem to exist is the selection of a portfolio of securities. Some participants in the stock market seem able to express definite opinions about the future course of a security. In this chapter let us assume that they can make comparisons between elements of R^* so that they have a distinct utility function and a distinct probability distribution over the possible states of the world. How will such an individual select a portfolio of securities? We examine this with some primitive examples.

selecting a portfolio
from a universe of two securities

An investor whose utility function for gain is $\log (x + 1)$ (where x is amount of gain) is faced with a universe consisting of only Security A and Security B. Assume he wishes to invest a fixed sum of money by purchasing some combination of A and B, in other words, he wishes to assemble a portfolio. The following table shows his subjective probability for the outcome of each security and the resultant expectant utility:

	PROFIT OUTCOME	PROBABILITY	EXPECTED UTILITY
SECURITY A	0 +30	$\frac{3}{4}$ $\frac{1}{4}$	$\frac{1}{4} \log (31) = 0.3729$
SECURITY B	0 +5	$\frac{1}{2}$ $\frac{1}{2}$	$\frac{1}{2} \log (6) = 0.3891$

If he were forced to make a choice between these two securities, he would choose Security B. Ordinarily he is not so constrained; he may invest a fraction of his capital in each security, or perhaps just one security, leaving the remainder in cash. In this instance, since he does not believe there is any possibility of loss, he will not wish to hold cash, but he must decide how to apportion his capital. Let p be the proportion of his capital invested in Security A, so that $1 - p$ is the proportion invested in Security B. If it is further assumed that the outcomes are independent, then a probability distribution of a portfolio can be tabulated:

PROFIT OUTCOME	PROB- ABILITY	EXPECTED UTILITY OF PORTFOLIO
$p(0) + (1 - p)(0) = 0$	$\frac{3}{8}$	$\frac{3}{8}[U(0)] + \frac{3}{8}[U(5 - 5p)] +$
$p(0) + (1 - p)(5)$	$\frac{3}{8}$	$\frac{1}{8}[U(30p)] + \frac{1}{8}[U(25p + 5)] =$
$p(30) + (1 - p)(0)$	$\frac{1}{8}$	$\frac{3}{8}\log(6 - 5p) + \frac{1}{8}\log(30p + 1) +$
$p(30) + (1 - p)(5)$	$\frac{1}{8}$	$\frac{1}{8}\log(25p + 6)$

In order to maximize expected utility, set $dE(U)/dp = -15/8(6 - 5p) + 30/8(30p + 1) + 25/8(25p + 6) = -3750p^2 + 980p + 228 = 0$, so that p is approximately 0.4. This investor would thus invest 40 per cent of his capital in Security A and 60 per cent in Security B and his probability distribution and expected utility would be:

PROFIT OUTCOME	PROBABILITY	EXPECTED UTILITY OF PORTFOLIO
0	$\frac{3}{8}$	$\frac{3}{8}\log 4 + \frac{1}{8}\log 13 + \frac{1}{8}\log 16$
3	$\frac{3}{8}$	$= 0.5155$
12	$\frac{1}{8}$	
15	$\frac{1}{8}$	

By considering a portfolio investments, the range of investment alternatives has been enlarged. By allowing short sales, opportunities are increasingly enriched, and not only in the obvious way. (A short sale allows an investor to profit from a fall in price in precisely the same way he can profit from a rise in price. If he sells short at $100 and it falls to $90, he gains $10; if it rises to $110, he loses $10.) To illustrate the subtle range of opportunity open to an investor able to engage in short sales, consider the universe consisting of only one common stock and its associated warrant. (A warrant is *an option to buy a stock*. The warrant is bought and sold like other securities. Under certain conditions the price of the warrant is determined completely by the price of the stock. Therefore, if an investor has some subjective expectation for the stock, this can be translated into a subjective expectation for the warrant.) By buying various amounts of common stock and warrants, an investor will have a large number of possible portfolios. But by buying common and shorting warrants, the set of possibilities is extended and it is very likely that in this extension lies a portfolio that maximizes expected utility beyond the *supremum* of the subset of portfolios consisting only of purchases.

For concreteness, consider how an investor whose utility function is $\log (x + 1)$ chooses a portfolio from a universe consisting only of the ABC common and the ABC warrant. The present price of the common is $10 and the warrant is $5. This investor's capital is $1500 and he wishes to select that portfolio which will maximize his utility.

His price expectations can be summarized:

SUBJECTIVE PROBABILITY	PRICE OF COMMON STOCK AT TIME t	RESULTING PRICE OF WARRANT AT TIME t
$\frac{1}{4}$	10	0
$\frac{1}{4}$	15	0
$\frac{1}{4}$	20	0
$\frac{1}{4}$	25	5

Assume first that this investor cannot sell short. Then he must decide how to apportion his $1500 among common stock, warrants, and cash. Since his expectations are that the warrant will not be above 5 at time t, he will not purchase any warrants for at best he will show no profit. On the other hand, since he believes that the common stock will not be below its present price at that time, he will not wish to hold cash, for the worst that can happen (in his view) if he holds only common is that he will show no profit. (For convenience it is now assumed that the rate of interest is 0.) Thus he will purchase 150 shares of common and the expected possible outcomes, their probability, and his expected utility become:

PRICE OF COMMON	PROFIT OUTCOME	PROB-ABILITY	EXPECTED UTILITY OF PORTFOLIO
25	$2250	$\frac{1}{4}$	$\frac{1}{4}\log 751 + \frac{1}{4}\log 150 +$
20	1500	$\frac{1}{4}$	$\frac{1}{4}\log 2251 = 2.3511$
15	750	$\frac{1}{4}$	
10	0	$\frac{1}{4}$	

Assume now that this investor is able to sell short so that he may apportion his $1500 between buying common and shorting warrants. Let p be the proportion of his capital devoted to purchasing common and $1 - p$ the proportion devoted to shorting warrants. His expected profit is a function of the price of the common:

PRICE OF COMMON	PRICE OF WARRANT	PROBABILITY	PROFIT OUTCOME
10	0	$\frac{1}{4}$	$1500 - 1500p$
15	0	$\frac{1}{4}$	$1500 - 750p$
20	0	$\frac{1}{4}$	1500
25	5	$\frac{1}{4}$	$2250p$

Expected profit if $p(1500)$ is invested in common at 10 and $(1 - p)(1500)$ is invested selling short warrants at 5.

His expected utility is $E(U) = \frac{1}{4}\log(1501 - 1500p) + \frac{1}{4}\log$ $(1501 - 750p) + \frac{1}{4}\log 1500$. Therefore, by setting $dE(U)/dp = 0$, it can be seen that his utility will be maximized when p is approximately 0.42, so that this investor will purchase 63 shares of common and sell short 174 warrants. With this portfolio the possible outcomes, their probability, and the utility of the portfolio become:

PRICE OF COMMON	PROFIT OUTCOME	PROB- ABILITY	EXPECTED UTILITY OF PORTFOLIO
10	870	$\frac{1}{4}$	$\frac{1}{4}\log 871 + \frac{1}{4}\log 1186 +$
15	1185	$\frac{1}{4}$	$\frac{1}{4}\log 1501 + \frac{1}{4}\log 946 =$
20	1500	$\frac{1}{4}$	3.0416
25	945	$\frac{1}{4}$	

Shorting warrants against purchases of common stock resembles an arbitrage operation—instead of a guaranteed profit regardless of the future course of prices, an investor who "hedges" by selling warrants and purchasing common usually *extends* the range in which future prices may profitably lie. This extension, coupled with a suitable subjective probability distribution, may yield a larger expected utility than otherwise possible. Warrants and other convertible securities appeal to many investors for precisely this reason. In the above example, by "hedging," this investor was able to increase his expected utility from 2.3511 to 3.0416.

Note that utility maximization resulted in a diversified portfolio—that is, a portfolio that did not specialize in any one security. If instead of maximizing utility an individual attempted to maximize expected return, he would simply choose that security which had the highest expected return. This behavior is rarely observed. Again, utility maximization, although a normative construct, might also be the basis for explaining how individuals actually behave.

efficient portfolios

In the real world, where thousands of securities are available to an individual investor, consciously maximizing a utility function is an almost impossible job. For this reason other techniques have been proposed. One concept that has given rise to much empirical and theoretical research is that of an "efficient portfolio," due to Markowitz (see Reference 1).

The riskiness of an asset, or a portfolio, hypothesized Markowitz, can be expressed by a measure called the *variance* of the return. Consider the following two securities with their subjective probability schedules:

SECURITY	RETURN	PROBABILITY
A	0%	$\frac{1}{2}$
	20%	$\frac{1}{2}$
B	-20%	$\frac{1}{2}$
	$+40\%$	$\frac{1}{2}$

Both securities have an expected return of 10 per cent but Security B has a larger range of possibilities—it is possible to lose more and gain more with B than with A, although on average both will return 10 per cent.

Suppose then, that investors consider not only expected return, but the variance of that return;[1] that for securities with the same expected return, the one with the least variance will be most preferred. For example, in the previous example, Security A will be preferred to B, and in general, of all the portfolios offering the same expected return, that portfolio with least variance will be

---

[1] The variance of a probability distribution is defined as the expected value of the squared differences from the mean. In symbols, $\operatorname{var}(X) = E\{[X - E(X)]^2\}$.

most preferred. Similarly, for all portfolios with the same variance, that one with greatest expected return will be most preferred.

In Fig. 5-1, the shaded area represents all the possible portfolios

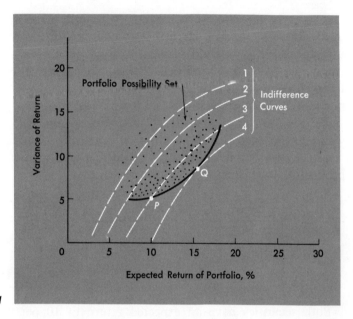

FIG. 5-1

available to an investor. The heavy curved line represents all the *efficient* portfolios in this set. For example, portfolio P has the smallest variance of all those portfolios with an expected return of 10 per cent. If expected return and variance are the only two characteristics that determine the suitability of a portfolio, then this investor may be willing to trade off higher return against higher variance, that is, he will accept a portfolio with larger variance but he must be compensated with a larger return. This suggests that he has an indifference map as indicated by the dashed lines in Fig. 4-1. The lower the curve, the more preferred the portfolios thereon. In thus attempting to maximize this utility function of expected return and variance, he will select that portfolio, of those available to him, that is tangent to his lowest indifference curve. He will select portfolio Q.

This technique has proved popular because many computational algorithms exist that can determine the efficient portfolio (given the investor's subjective expectations). Thus, when confronted with this efficient portfolio, his area of choice having been limited enormously, it is presumably easier to decide on the best portfolio.

What is the connection between efficient portfolio selection and utility maximization in general? It can be shown (see Ref. 1, pp. 286–87) that they are entirely equivalent in the case where the individual's utility function for gain is a quadratic function of the form $U(R) = aR + bR^2 + c$. Of course many curvilinear relations can be well approximated by a quadratic function, and in these cases, efficient portfolio selection can be a very useful approximation to utility maximization. Thus portfolio-selection theory may be viewed as an improvement over the criterion of maximizing expected value which is equivalent to maximizing a linear-utility function—the improvement due to the introduction of quadratic rather than linear-utility functions.

But we must not forget that the quadratic utility function has many unpleasant properties:

1. Beyond some finite gain it is monotonic decreasing implying negative-marginal utility
2. An increase in wealth, no matter how great, will not result in the increase of purchase of a risky asset, characterizing risky assets as inferior goods[2]
3. It cannot discriminate between skewed distributions; a quadratic utility function ranks the following two assets as equally desirable: Asset A with 0.1 probability of 80 per cent loss and 0.9 probability of 20 per cent gain, and Asset B with 0.1 probability of 100 per cent gain and 0.9 probability of

[2] See John Pratt, "Risk Aversion in the Small and in the Large," *Econometrica*, 32, No. 1-2 (1964), pp. 122–136.

0 per cent gain. Both assets have expected value of 10 per cent and standard deviation of return of 30 per cent, but most investors would not view them equally desirable[3]

PROBLEMS

1. Calculate and draw the efficiency set of portfolios consisting of cash and one asset which has an expected return of 10 per cent and a variance of return of 10 per cent.

2. The same as Problem 1 but instead of cash, consider a riskless investment (say government bonds) with zero variance and return of 3 per cent.

3. Show that if 2 assets have independent returns, even though one asset may have a higher return *and* a lower variance, it is possible that some *combination* is more efficient than the superior asset.

REFERENCES

1. MARKOWITZ, H. M., *Portfolio Selection*. New York: John Wiley & Sons, Inc., 1959.   Markowitz wrote the seminal article on portfolio selection theory in 1952; this book is a complete statement of that early exposition.

2. SHARPE, W. F., "A Simplified Model for Portfolio Analysis," *Management Science*, 9, (1963), pp. 277–293.   The introduction of a computational simplification that makes the Markowitz model accessible.

3. *Journal of Financial and Quantitative Analysis*, June 1967.   This entire issue is devoted to portfolio analysis and contains articles by W. F. Sharpe, B. A. Wallingford, P. A. Samuelson, E. F. Renshaw, A. E. Hofflandes, Jr., R. M. Duval, J. B. Michaelsen and R. C. Goshay.

[3] This example is taken from Howard Raiffa's brilliant *Decision Analysis* (Reading, Mass.: Addison-Wesley Publishing Company, Inc., 1968), p. 56.

IN THE ABSENCE
OF PROBABILITIES
CHAPTER SIX

The decision situation can be generalized in many directions. Until now it has been assumed that the decision maker has clear-cut preferences among strategies. Let us continue to assume that his preferences among pure strategies (strategies leading to unequivocal outcomes) are still consistent and transitive, but that when he leaves the world of certainty he cannot express consistent preferences among strategies because of his total ignorance of the states of the world. For example, upon arriving in a foreign country about which he knows nothing, a decision maker may be asked to choose from a list of 5 candidates the one most likely to win an election. Because he has no prior knowledge or experience in this situation he may not be able to express any preference among lotteries involving the candidates. Thus we will not be able to deduce his subjective probabilities for the states of the world.

As might be expected, there is no completely satisfactory way to handle these situations. After all, if the decision maker does not know his own mind, it is difficult to advise what is "best" for him. But because many decision makers perceive themselves to be in exactly this position, many criteria have been proposed for making choices in this situation. We will examine some of these criteria along with their shortcomings.

the principle of indifference

If there are n possible states of the world and a decision maker has no prior knowledge, intuition, or experience concerning these states, then perhaps he should assign equal probability to each state, i.e., assign probability $1/n$ to each state of the world, and then select that strategy with greatest expected utility. This is the criterion dictated by the so-called *principle of indifference;* it is also called the *Laplace criterion.* At first blush, this is intuitively compelling. But it has been under constant attack since first proposed by James Bernoulli. "No other formula in the alchemy of logic has exerted more astonishing powers. For it has established the existence of God from the premise of total ignorance." [1]

A simple example will indicate the difficulties to which this criterion may lead. Suppose you arrived in a country of which you know nothing and are given the following facts: the population ranges in age from 0 to 100, and everyone's income is exactly the square of his age. In particular, you have no knowledge concerning the distribution of ages. A name is selected at random from

[1] J. M. Keynes, *A Treatise on Probability* (New York: Harper and Row, Publishers, 1962), p. 82.

the census files and you wish to assign a probability that the person selected is less than 50 years of age. The indifference principle leads you to assign probability $\frac{1}{2}$. Call this Situation 1.

Suppose instead that you wished to assign a probability to the statement that the selected individual had an income of less than $5,000. You know only that incomes range from $0 to $10,000. The indifference principle leads you to assign probability $\frac{1}{2}$ to this statement. Because of the connection between age and income, this is entirely equivalent to saying that the probability is $\frac{1}{2}$ that the selected individual is less than 70.7107 years of age ($70.7^2 =$ $5,000). This contradicts the assignment of probabilities arrived at in Situation 1.

Figure 6-1 illustrates the difficulty. This criterion asserts that since nothing is known about the distribution of age in this

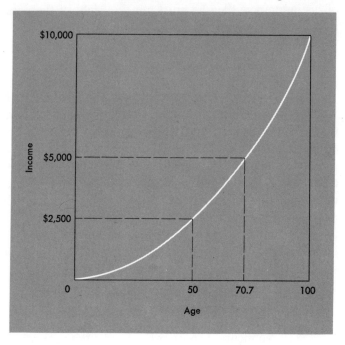

FIG. 6-1

country, we should assume the uniform distribution, that is, the distribution which assigns equal probability to every age. Similarly, since nothing is known about the distribution of income, we should assign the uniform distribution to income. But since age and income are not related linearly, a uniform probability distribution for age implies a nonuniform-probability distribution for income, and vice-versa.

In spite of this, and other difficulties (Keynes, *ibid.*, Chap. 4) this criterion has many supporters. The nub of the difficulty lies in defining states of the world that have equal probability. If the decision maker truly believes that the states are equally probable, then he *has* specific consistent preferences among strategies involving lotteries and he is not in a state of "complete ignorance." On the other hand, if he is applying equal probabilities only because of his ignorance, then he must not lose sight of the possibility of paradoxical behavior.

the maxi-min criterion

A defensive, pessimistic decision maker, perhaps one who has never won a contest, invariably finds himself in the wrong line at supermarkets, and whose choice of entree is always less appetizing than his wife's, might decide on the following criterion: for each available strategy consider only the worst possible outcome; then choose that strategy with the best of these worst outcomes, that is, maximize the minimum outcome. This is the *maxi-min criterion*. This criterion implies that the world is against the decision maker. No matter which strategy he selects, he believes he will be dealt the worst possible outcome. Under most circumstances, this appears to be too cautious a stance.

the maxi-max criterion

An incurable optimist, one who conveniently forgets all his losses and remembers only his gains in the stock market, one whose recollections of Las Vegas consist entirely of those winning passes, one whose faith in the goodness of the world is unbounded, might choose the following sanguine criterion: For each available strategy consider only the best possible outcome; then choose that strategy with the best of these best outcomes, that is, maximize the maximum outcome. This is the *maxi-max criterion*. Most decision makers would consider this too audacious.

the hurwicz-optimism index

The maxi-min and maxi-max criteria are extreme cases of a more generalized criterion. Hurwicz has asked, why concentrate on only the best outcome (maxi-max) or worst outcome (maxi-min) associated with each strategy? By taking some weighted average of the best and worst outcomes he proposed an index of optimism that would not necessarily categorize the decision maker as a hopeless pessimist or total optimist. To illustrate his criterion, consider the following decision situation where the entries in the matrix represent the utility of the payoff:

MATRIX 6.1:

	W_1	W_2	W_3
S_1	10	0	-1.2
S_2	8	4	0
S_3	3	3	3

A decision maker using the maxi-max criterion would select S_1, since this strategy will yield the greatest payoff if God is in His heaven. On the other hand, the maxi-min criterion would select S_3, since the worst the decision maker can experience is a payoff of 3, which is greater than the other "worsts." Hurwicz argues that each individual's temperament probably lies somewhere between total optimism and pessimism. This can be expressed by looking at the best *and* worst outcomes associated with each strategy and taking some weighted average. Call the weight given to the worst outcome, α, a number between 0 and 1, so that the weight given to the best outcome is $1 - \alpha$. For example, if $\alpha = 0.2$, we weight the best and worst outcomes associated with strategy 1 by: $0.2(-1.2) + 0.8(10) = 7.76$, which is called the α index of S_1. Thus, with each strategy is associated an α index. The criterion then dictates that the strategy with the highest index should be selected. Note that if $\alpha = 0$, this criterion is equivalent to the maxi-max criterion and if $\alpha = 1$, it is equivalent to the maxi-min criterion.

Let m_i be the worst outcome possible if S_i is chosen and M_i the best outcome. Then the α index associated with each S_i is $\alpha m_i + (1 - \alpha)M_i = M_i + \alpha(m_i - M_i)$. In the above example, the α indices would be

$$S_1: \quad 10 - 11.2\alpha$$
$$S_2: \quad 8 - 8\alpha$$
$$S_3: \quad 3$$

The α index is a linear function of α. For the above situation, the graphs of the indices are plotted in Fig. 6-2. If the decision maker's α is less than $\frac{5}{8}$, then S_1 is the superior strategy; if α is greater than $\frac{5}{8}$, S_3 is the superior strategy. For no value of α is S_2 a preferred strategy. Therefore, in running the gamut from pessimist ($\alpha = 1$) to optimist ($\alpha = 0$), the Hurwicz criterion would never rank strategy 2 as the superior choice. We next consider a criterion that *does* choose S_2 as the superior strategy, indicating the not so satisfactory state of affairs when probabilities cannot be assigned to the states of the world.

the savage regret criterion

Investors in Wall Street must constantly select strategies. Judging by a small biased sample of conversations at cocktail

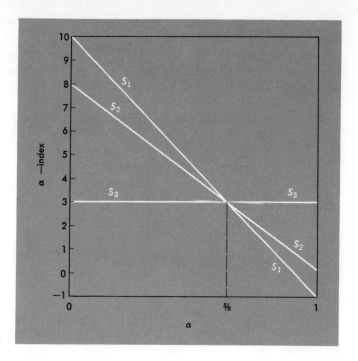

FIG. 6-2

parties it appears that often the buyer of a stock will elect to sell his shares after they have moved up, perhaps to double their cost price, only to see them move up even more sharply after they have been sold. If the proceeds of the sale have been reinvested in a situation that remains relatively stagnant, the investor experiences definite pain and discomfort; hence the many tales of how rich an investor would have been if he hadn't sold his IBM stock. Savage (Ref. 4 on p. 54) attempts to deal with the anguish resulting from guessing wrong, or, choosing the wrong strategy. Consider once more the decision situation given by Matrix 6.1. Assume the true state of the world is W_1. If S_2 is selected, the decision maker may regret that he did not choose S_1, for then he would have gained a utility of 10 rather than 8. If he selected S_3, his regret would be stronger—there was a possibility of gaining a utility of 10 rather than the 3 he experienced by choosing S_3. Let a_{ij}, measure his regret by the difference between his maximum utility given the ith state of the world and the utility received from selecting S_j. The resulting matrix of these differences is called the *regret matrix*. The regret matrix for Matrix 6.1 is shown as Matrix 6.2.

MATRIX 6.2: *Savage Regret Matrix for Decision Situation of Matrix 6.1*

	W_1	W_2	W_3
S_1	0	4	4.2
S_2	2	0	3
S_3	7	1	0

In a sense, the entries in the regret matrix represent the "cost" of guessing nonoptimally. A decision maker is concerned with minimizing his cost. If he were cautious (or pessimistic, or overly defensive) he might decide to minimize his maximum possible loss. That is, he would rank each strategy by its maximum possible loss and select that strategy with the smallest such maximum. Thus S_1 has a maximum possible loss of 4.2, S_2 of 3, and S_3 of 7. This would rank S_2 as more preferred than S_1 which in turn is more preferred than S_3. This procedure of selecting the strategy which minimizes the maximum possible loss (regret) is called the *savage regret criterion*.

Note that for the decision situation of Matrix 6.1, the maxi-min Criterion selects S_3, the maxi-max criterion S_1, and the Savage regret criterion S_2. To confuse matters further, there is no a priori reason why the regret matrix could not be used with some sort of α index, rather than resorting to the most pessimistic view.

Thus in the absence of probabilities it has not been possible to demonstrate that there exists a "best" strategy for the decision maker. The difficulty arises because we have defined "best" to mean most preferred by the decision maker and in the case of complete ignorance concerning the states of the world, the decision maker is unable to rank all possible alternatives consistently. This is an unhappy state for an "expert." When convinced that the decision maker is truly operating in complete ignorance of the state of the world, he can offer conflicting advice depending upon selection of criterion.

PROBLEMS

1. Consider the following decision situation where nothing is known about the probabilities of the states of the world.

	W_1	W_2	W_3	W_4
S_1	12	3	6	6
S_2	10	0	10	10
S_3	5	4	5	5
S_4	18	0	4	3

    a. Which strategy would the Laplace criterion select; the maxi-max criterion; the mini-max criterion?

    b. Graph the α index for each strategy as a function of α. For which values of α will S_1 be selected?

REFERENCES

1. See the references for Chap. 5.

2. THRALL, R. M., C. H. COOMBS, AND R. L. DAVIS, eds., *Decision Processes.* New York: John Wiley & Sons, Inc., 1954.   In particular, see the articles by L. A. Goodman, J. Milnor, and R. Radner and J. Marschak.

FURTHER GENERALIZATIONS
CHAPTER SEVEN

strategy selection under conflict

In operating without probabilities, there is one special case that has been examined extensively—decision situations involving an opponent rather than a state of the world. This area of decision making is known as game theory. We begin by considering a 2-person game: a decision maker and one opponent. The decision maker is player 1 and his opponent player 2. Assume further that the decision maker and his opponent are in complete

conflict concerning the outcome. (At the other extreme both may
be in complete agreement, in which case the decision maker and
his opponent will obviously choose the strategy which simultaneously maximizes each one's utility.) If both players know all
strategies available to each other the game can be characterized
by a matrix. As an example:

MATRIX 7.1: *A Game Between a Decision Maker and an Opponent*

	W_1	W_2	W_3	W_4
S_1	9	2	0	8
S_2	5	4	5	5
S_3	3	1	6	4

In Matrix 7.1 the decision maker must choose between strategies
S_1, S_2, and S_3. His opponent must choose between W_1, W_2, W_3, or
W_4. The entries in the matrix represent the utility of the outcome
to the decision maker, since we assume this to be a case of complete
conflict, they also represent the *disutility* to the opponent. For
example, these entries might be the money payoff that the opponent must make to the decision maker where both have linear
utility functions for money. Thus if the decision maker chooses S_1
and his opponent W_4, then the opponent pays the decision maker
$8. This case of complete conflict where one player's gain is
exactly equal to the other's loss is called a *zero-sum game*. When
facing an opponent rather than states of the world, the decision
maker may decide to select the strategy that will yield the greatest
return in *view of the opponent's possibilities*. The military strategy
of the United States is said to be based on this criterion.[1] Rather
than try to predict what the enemy will do (attach probabilities
to his strategies), a military commander selects a strategy on the
basis of the punishment the enemy is able to inflict on his forces.

[1] See O. G. Haywood, Jr., "Military Decision and Game Theory," *Journal
of the Operations Research Society of America*, 2, (1954), pp. 365–385.

This is equivalent to selecting a strategy by invoking the maxi-min criterion. It is important to keep in mind that nothing in game theory points to the maxi-min criterion as the "best" method of analysis for the decision maker—it is *assumed* that the decision maker has already chosen this criterion. It has been previously noted that this is a cautious, defensive posture. Under conflict with a malevolent opponent in a zero-sum game this criterion has much appeal. For the remainder of this chapter we assume that this criterion is chosen to guide the decision maker.

If both players of the game depicted in Matrix 6.3 use the maxi-min criterion what will be the outcome? First, the decision maker will select S_2 since this maximizes the minimum payoff, and he is sure to receive at least 4. His opponent, wishing to minimize his loss will select W_2 since this minimizes his maximum payoff. The outcome will be that the decision maker receives 4 from his opponent. Note that if the decision maker chooses S_2 and his opponent does *not* choose W_2, the decision maker receives more than 4; similarly if the opponent chooses W_2 and the decision maker does *not* choose S_2 the opponent will have a loss of less than 4. Since both players know each other's alternatives, and since both are invoking the cautious maxi-min criterion, there will be no incentive for either of them to veer from choosing S_2 and W_2. In this particular case, the outcome is said to be in equilibrium. It is not difficult to show that an outcome is in equilibrium if, and only if, it is the minimum entry in its row and the maximum entry in its column. (See Prob. 1.)

A 2-person zero-sum game may not have an equilibrium outcome. For example:

MATRIX 7.1: *A Game with No Equilibrium Solution*

	W_1	W_2
S_1	3	1
S_2	2	4

In this game, the decision maker would choose S_2 by the maxi-min criterion, since he is then assured a gain of at least 2. His opponent would choose W_1, since he is then assured of paying out at most 3. But since the decision maker knows his opponent's choice based on the maxi-min criterion he would then be motivated to choose S_1 to increase his return to 3. Similarly, his opponent can also follow this reasoning and so instead would choose W_2. As a result, there is no equilibrium outcome to this game. But von Neumann's celebrated theorem proves that there *is* a pair of strategies that will be in equilibrium for every 2-person zero-sum game if randomized strategies, rather than only pure strategies are allowed. *A randomized strategy* is one that places a probability on each available strategy rather than a straight or pure selection. For example, a randomized strategy might be: choose S_1 if the flip of an unbiased coin results in a head, otherwise choose S_2. The proof of this theorem and further consequences of 2-person zero-sum games will not be developed here. Instead we consider next a generalization which seems to face many decision makers.

nonzero-sum games

Zero-sum games do not capture the vitality of many actual situations. With the possible exception of some parlor games, one player's gain seldom equals the other's loss. Even in a simple game between an adult and a child, the child's gain may actually represent a gain in utility for the adult who loses purposely. This is an outcome in which both players gain a positive utility.

There is one vexing nonzero-sum game that has received much attention. It is called the prisoner's dilemma. We illustrate this situation with a different interpretation from the traditional one, which gave rise to its name. Consider a "game" between two world powers. The decision maker for one world power must choose between the following two strategies:

S_1: Disarm and divert resources to constructing water desalinization plants

S_2: Continue to arm at the present rate

His opponent, representing the other power, must choose between W_1 and W_2 which represent the same strategies available to the decision maker of Power 1. If the outcomes are described by the billions of dollars gained or lost by each power, the game can be represented by the following matrix:

MATRIX 7.2: *Nuclear Power Nonzero-sum Game*

	W_1	W_2
S_1	(50, 50)	(−110, 60)
S_2	(60, −110)	(−50, −50)

Since this is a nonzero-sum game, each entry in the matrix must show the gain to each player. The first number in each parentheses represents the gain to Power 1 and the second number the gain to Power 2.

To rationalize these entries, let us consider the four possible cases. (S_1, W_1): Both powers disarm. The payoff to each is $50 billion, the benefits of desalinization. (S_1, W_2): The decision maker disarms and his opponent continues to arm. Power 2 takes over Power 1 since it is now able to do so. The effect on Power 1 is a loss of $110 billion, perhaps in goods and services it must give to Power 2. The payoff to Power 2 is $60 billion, since it must still subject Power 1 to military sanction and the $50 billion armament cost deducted from the $110 billion leaves a payoff of $60 billion. (S_2, W_1): The same as the previous case with the position of the powers reversed. (S_2, W_2): Both continue to arm with each receiving a negative payoff of $50 billion. In this last case, their negative payoff is actually greater than the cost of armament since now the probability of war increases, in which case both will suffer additional expected costs. To illustrate the dilemma it is not necessary to consider this additional cost.

The decision maker analyzes the situation in this manner: if the opponent selects W_1 my optimal strategy is S_2 since 60 exceeds 50; if the opponent selects W_2 my optimal strategy is again S_2. His opponent, in a completely symmetrical argument, decides that his optimal strategy is W_2. Thus with 2 "rational" players, the outcome of the game is a loss of $50 billion for each.

The preceding analysis has assumed that there was no collusion between both powers. If communication exists between the two players it seems likely that they could reach an agreement of bilateral disarmament, since this represents an outcome that is better for both. If communication or cooperation is not possible, or if a similar situation involves "many" players, then the "best" outcome for all players will probably not result, since it will then be in each player's self-interest to choose to arm. (This decision situation is called the *prisoner's dilemma* because in its original formulation it involved 2 prisoners who were *not* in communication with each other and who had to choose between confessing or not confessing, realizing that the other was faced with exactly the same strategies.)

In a many-person game involving the prisoner's dilemma the outcome will be suboptimal if each player seeks his own self interest. (Suboptimal means that there exists another outcome which will improve at least one player's payoff without reducing that of any other player.) These games are "unfair" because if some players act in the common good, but others do not, the "good" guys finish last. In these situations, some apparatus is needed to coerce each player into acting differently than "rationality" dictates. In the "game" of international politics, Kenneth Boulding makes an eloquent appeal for strengthening supranational institutions to the point where they can coerce players into optimal behavior. "Indeed, for the meagre resources that we devote to the international order (e.g., the United Nations), we get a remarkable return. This becomes apparent when we consider that the combined budget for all the international agencies is less than that of the Ford Foundation." [2]

collective decision making

Individuals do not have a monopoly on decision making. Groups of individuals—members of clubs, boards of directors, citizens of a state, must frequently select a strategy from some available set. If all members of the group have the same preferences and probability estimates, then the situation is identical with individual decision making—any member of the group can be considered the decision maker for the group. His strategy selection will be unanimously endorsed by the others.

In cases where the individual members of the group have different preferences, the situation is quite different. A group may select a strategy by tradition, in which people who have always acted in a certain manner shall continue to do so; or by allowing some one individual (father, chairman, king) to decide for the group. We in the Western world are suspicious of this last procedure. We are fearful that the individual deciding for the group may not be benevolent or wise—or worse, that he may behave selfishly. The "fair" solution that first comes to mind is to resort to majority rule to express the preferences of the group. Unfortunately, in a situation involving at least 3 strategies, majority rule sometimes leads to inconsistent choices. For example, suppose a group of three individuals, I_1, I_2, and I_3 must choose a strategy from the available set S_1, S_2, and S_3. The following tabulation shows the individual preferences of each individual, with his most preferred strategy at the top of the column and his least preferred at the bottom.

[2] Kenneth E. Boulding, "The Learning and Reality-Testing Process in the International System," *Journal of International Affairs*, (1967), XXI, pp. 1-15.

I_1	I_2	I_3
S_1	S_2	S_3
S_2	S_3	S_1
S_3	S_1	S_2

For example, Individual 3 prefers S_3 to S_1 and S_1 to S_2. If majority rule is to dictate the group's preferences among the strategies, we have the following: $S_1 \geq S_2$ (where $\geq$ again denotes preference) since both I_1 and I_3 prefer S_1 to S_2; $S_2 \geq S_3$ since I_1 and I_2 prefer S_2 to S_3; and $S_3 \geq S_1$ since I_2 and I_3 prefer S_3 to S_1. This is an intransitive ordering, because with $S_1 \geq S_2$ and $S_2 \geq S_3$, transitivity requires that $S_1 \geq S_3$, which is not the case with majority rule.

This intransitivity would lead to the choice of any one of the strategies depending upon the order in which choice between pairs is taken. For example, if the three individuals are asked to choose first between S_1 and S_2, with the winner of this round to compete against S_3, the final choice will be S_3. If however, they are asked to first choose between S_3 and S_1 with the winner pitted against S_2, the final choice will be S_2. Similarly, if the first round is between S_2 and S_3, the final choice will be S_1. Thus the final choice of majority rule is completely arbitrary and depends upon the manner in which the first round of candidates is presented. An intransitive preference structure violates our "rationality" axioms because it leads to inconsistencies of this type.

This example is known as the *Arrow paradox*, after Kenneth Arrow (see Ref. 1). Arrow has shown that if a group's preference structure is to maintain certain "reasonable" conditions then we cannot count on majority rule to lead to a "reasonable" preference ranking for the group. We will not consider the "reasonable" conditions that Arrow contends should be imposed on a group preference; although they have been criticized and analyzed in many places (see especially Ref. 3, Appendix 2). Instead, we will examine the conditions necessary for majority rule to lead to a "reasonable" solution, that is, a transitive, group preference ranking. Since majority rule is so firmly entrenched in our institutional procedures it is well to know when it may lead to paradoxical results.

Suppose an odd numbered group had to select a strategy from the available set of S_1, S_2, S_3, and S_4. There are 24 ways in which an individual can rank these strategies. If some of these 24 ways never arise, it can be shown that majority rule will lead to a transitive group ordering of preference. A graph can illustrate which individual preference rankings are admissible in order that majority rule leads to rational collective preferences.

In Fig. 7-1 the available strategies have been located on a linear scale. If each individual in the group viewed each strategy as having more or less of some attribute which determines its attractiveness and the degree of this attribute determines the strategy's position on the line, the position of the four strategies might be as indicated in Fig. 7-1. For example, the 4 strategies might repre-

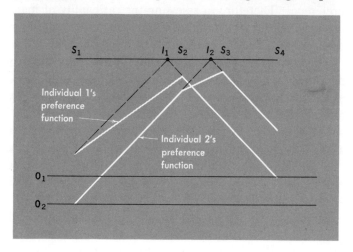

FIG. 7-1

sent the choice of 1 of 4 candidates, with each candidate having some amount of liberal quality—the further a candidate is to the left on the line the more liberal he is, and the further to the right the more conservative. Suppose Individual 1, I_1, had some ideal amount of liberalism or conservatism he wished to see in a candidate, and ranked available candidates by the amount they deviated from this ideal. In Fig. 7-1, suppose the point marked I_1 represents this individual's ideal. Then by projecting the position of the available strategies upon the two 45° dashed lines emanating from I_1 we can indicate the preference structure of I_1. If we number his least preferred strategy 0_1, and use this as a base line from which we measure his preference for the other strategies, we see that his preference function indicated by the heavy line rises to a peak at S_2 and falls away monotonically from this peak. Similarly, if Individual 2 has an ideal at the point marked I_2, his preference function will have a peak at S_3 and fall away monotonically on both sides. If all individuals in the group have single peaked preference functions, that is, have some ideal along the line and rank strategies by their distance from the ideal, then Black (Ref. 2) has shown that majority voting will lead to a transitive group preference. Therefore in assessing the rationality of majority voting it is helpful to determine if only single-peak preference functions characterize the individuals in the group.

Musgrave (Ref. 6) has shown that if certain tax and expenditure decisions are decided by majority rule the outcome *could* be arbitrary. And yet political processes based upon majority rule do not appear to be chaotic, suggesting that individuals in these societies have fairly similar preferences, ranking their alternatives along some continuum. When the alternatives possess more than one attribute that is relevant to the ranking, that is, when the alternatives are positioned in more than one dimension, the arbitrary quality of majority rule is likely to rise.

Majority rule carries with it the implicit assumption that each voter's satisfaction in winning is equal to every other voter's. If this is true, then majority rule achieves the greatest total satisfaction. This assumption concerning the comparison of utilities between individuals is suspect and questioned by many. Clearly, intensity of preference must vary greatly when choosing between some alternatives—I may barely prefer Candidate A to Candidate

B whereas you may violently oppose A and embrace B; but my vote counts as much as yours.

Thus a political process using majority rule is a rather crude way of registering the preferences of the individuals comprising a group. This is especially so when the procedure is compared with an economic solution in a free enterprise situation where each individual's preferences is registered very finely. Nevertheless, some qualifications must be made about this comparison. First, since voters with intense preferences are free to persuade, they may have more influence than voters with weak preferences. Second, an economic solution, although efficient, may be "unfair" because it is dependent upon the distribution of income. For example, the market solution in Saudi Arabia is not necessarily superior to a nonmarket solution in a more egalitarian society. (For a thorough treatment of the welfare aspects of the market solution see Ref. 5.)

In this chapter we have generalized the decision making process in two ways. First by considering an "opponent" rather than a neutral state of the world. Only by imposing a further criterion, namely, the maxi-min criterion, could we specify the "best" course of action. Second, by considering the decision of a group. It was seen that majority rule is not sine qua non for rational group decision making. There is at least one further generalization that could be considered, the case where the decision maker may not even know all the alternatives available to him. We have implicitly assumed throughout that the set of alternatives were known to the decision maker. In practice, this is seldom the case.

An architect, confronted with a site, a family, and a budget, cannot even conceptually enumerate or define the alternative house designs available. Instead he searches for a solution as if moving in a maze: he arrives at cul-de-sacs and he back tracks; he arrives at junctures that do not seem promising and he retraces his steps to some previous position so that he can move out along a new path. At some point he stops and presents his "solution." The solution may satisfy all the imposed constraints but it would be a miracle if it were "optimal." This same difficulty faces city planners, political rulers, composers, and business men. Are there any principles or theories to guide us in these search procedures? This is an area now receiving much attention and which will probably have the greatest practical application. For a path-breaking discussion, see Ref. 8, Chap. 3.

PROBLEMS

1. Show that in a 2-person zero-sum game an outcome in the decision matrix is an equilibrium outcome if, and only if, it is the minimum value in its row and the maximum value in its column.

2. Construct a game which has more than one equilibrium solution.

3. In Fig. 7-1, suppose that the distance between S_1 and S_2 is 5; between S_2 and S_3 is 2; between S_3 and S_4 is 3. Write all the possible ways in which an individual can rank S_1 through S_4; which of these possible rankings are single-peaked?

REFERENCES

1. ARROW, K., *Social Choice and Individual Values*. New York: John Wiley & Sons, Inc., 1951.

2. BLACK, D., "The Decisions of a Committee Using a Special Majority," *Econometrica*, 16, (1948), pp. 245–261.

3. BUCHANAN, J. M., AND TULLOCK, G., *The Calculus of Consent*. Ann Arbor: University of Michigan Press, 1962.

4. DOWNS, A., *Economic Theory of Democracy*. New York: Harper & Row, Publishers, 1957.

5. GRAAF, J. DE V., *Theoretical Welfare Economics*. New York: Cambridge University Press, 1957.

6. MUSGRAVE, R. A., *The Theory of Public Finance*, Chapter 6, New York: McGraw-Hill, Inc., 1959.

7. SCHELLING, T. C., *The Strategy of Conflict*. New York: Oxford University Press, Inc., 1963.

8. SIMON, H. A., *The Sciences of the Artificial*. Cambridge: The M.I.T. Press, 1969.

INDEX

Affluent Society, The, 1
Anscombe, F. J., 53
Arrow, K., 86
Arrow paradox, 82
Aumann, R. J., 53

Barzun, J., 1
Bernoulli, D., 38
Bernoulli, J., 66
Black, D., 86
Boulding, K., 80, 81
Buchanan, J. M., 86
Budget line, defined, 11

Calculus of Consent, The, 86
Collective decisions, 81–85
Consumer decision problem, 8–16

Debreu, G., 14
Decision Analysis, 64
Decision and Value Theory, 43
Decision Processes, 14, 73
Decision situation, defined, 5
   under certainty, 6
   collective, 81–85
   under conflict, 75–80
   with objective probabilities, 26–27, 30
   with subjective probabilities, 47–48

"Decisions of a Committee Using a
   Special Majority, The," 86
"Definition of Subjective Probability,
   A," 53
Diet problem, 17–21
Downs, A., 86
Duval, R. M., 64

Economic Theory of Democracy, 86
Efficient portfolios, 62
Equilibrium outcome, 77
Equivalence class of outcomes, 13
Expected utility, defined, 36
Expected value, 28

Fishburn, P. C., 43
Foundations of Mathematics, The, 54
Foundations of Statistics, The, 54

Galbraith, J. K., 1
Gale, D., 22
Games and Decisions, 43, 54
Game theory, 75–80
Goodman, L. A., 73
Goshay, R. C., 64
Graaf, J. de V., 86

Haywood, O. G., Jr., 76
Hedging, 60
Henderson, J. M., 23
Hofflandes, A. E., Jr., 64
House of Intellect, The, 1
Hurwicz criterion, 69–70

Indifference curve, defined, 10
  portfolio selection, 62–63
Indifference map, defined, 10

Keynes, J. M., 66, 68

Lagrangian multiplier, 13, 15, 22, 23
Laplace criterion, 66
"Learning and Reality-Testing Process
  in the International System, The,"
  81
Lincar programming, 15, 22
Luce, R. D., 43, 45

Majority rule, 81–85
Markowitz, H., 61, 64
Marschak, J., 73
Mathematical expectation, 28
Maxi-max criterion, 68
Maxi-min criterion, 68
Michaelson, J. B., 64
Microeconomic Theory, 22
"Military Decision and Game Theory,"
  76
Milnor, J., 73
Morgenstern, O., 43
Musgrave, R., 84, 86

Nonzero-sum games, 78–81
Normative theory, 1, 2

Outcome:
  under certainty, 6
  equilibrium, 77
  equivalent, 13
  with objective probabilities, 27

Petersburg paradox, 29
  resolution, 38–41
Portfolio, efficient, 62
Portfolio Selection, 56–64
Portfolio selection, 64
Pratt, J., 63
Principle of indifference, 66
Prisoner's dilemma, 78–81
Probability:
  objective, 26, 27
  subjective, 45–47
*Probability and Statistics for Business
  Decisions*, 54

Quandt, R. E., 23

Radner, R., 73
Raiffa, H., 43, 54, 64
Ramsey, F. P., 54
Randomized strategy, 78
Rational behavior, 2, 7
  axioms under certainty, 7
  axioms with objective probabilities,
    31–33, 35
Renshaw, E. F., 64
Risk, 30
"Risk Aversion in the Small and in the
  Large," 63

Samuelson, P. A., 64
Savage, L. J., 54
Savage regret criterion, 70–72
Schelling, T. C., 86
Schlaiffer, R., 54
Sciences of the Artificial, The, 86
Sharpe, W. F., 64
Short sale, 58
Simon, H. A., 4, 86
"Simplified Model for Portfolio Analy-
  sis, A," 64
Social Choice and Individual Values, 86
States of the world, 47–48
Strategy:
  under certainty, 6
  compound, 33
  under conflict, 75–80
  pure, 31
  randomized, 78
Strategy of Conflict, The, 86

Theoretical Welfare Economics, 86
Theory of Games and Economic Behavior,
  43
Theory of Linear Economic Models, The,
  22
Theory of Public Finance, The, 86
Treatise on Probability, A, 66, 68
Tullock, G., 86

Utility, 32
  expected, 36
Utility function:
  cardinal, 36–37
  ordinal, 13–14

Variance, 61
Von Neumann, J., 43

Wallingford, B. A., 64
Warrant, 58

Zero-sum game, 76